THE HOLY SPIRIT

THE HOLY SPIRIT

MARIA WOODWORTH-ETTER

WHITAKER
HOUSE

Editor's note: *The Holy Spirit* is a collection of Maria Woodworth-Etter's sermons, originally titled *Holy Ghost Sermons*. It has been edited for clarity and readability, with dated words, expressions, and sentence structure updated for the modern reader.

THE HOLY SPIRIT

ISBN: 0-88368-548-5
Printed in the United States of America
Copyright © 1998 by Whitaker House

Whitaker House
30 Hunt Valley Circle
New Kensington, PA 15068

Library of Congress Cataloging-in-Publication Data

Woodworth-Etter, Maria Beulah, 1844–1924.
  The Holy Spirit / by Maria Woodworth-Etter.
    p. cm.
  ISBN 0-88368-548-5 (trade paper)
  1. Holy Spirit. 2. Christian life—Pentecostal authors. I. Title.
BT122.W65 1998
231'.3—dc21   98-38595

2 3 4 5 6 7 8 9 10 11 12 / 09 08 07 06 05 04 03 02

Contents

Early Life and Experience in the Work

I was born in New Lisbon, Ohio, on July 22, 1844, the fourth daughter of Samuel Underwood. My parents were not Christians, but when I was ten years old, they joined the Disciples' Church. One year later, my father, who was a drunkard, got struck by lightning in a terrible storm and died. It was an awful blow to all our young hearts to see our father carried cold and stiff into the house and our mother fainting as fast as they could bring her to. There were eight of us children, and soon my older sisters and I had to go out and work to provide for the family. I longed for an education, but this seemed impossible.

At the age of thirteen, I attended a meeting that a Dr. Belding was holding. When I heard the story of the Cross, my heart was filled with the love of Jesus and my eyes were like a fountain of tears. When the invitation to seek God was given, I was the first one to respond. It seemed so far to the front, but I said,

> I can't but perish if I go,
> I am resolved to try,
> For if I stay away I know
> I shall forever die.

The Holy Spirit

The minister took a great interest in me and said many things to encourage me. If he could have looked forward and seen my lifework for the Master, he would have rejoiced to know how kindly he had spoken to the poor little orphan girl. But I did not get fully converted then. The next day, as they took me down to the creek to baptize me, I heard someone say, "Maybe she will be drowned." It scared me a little. I thought, "Maybe I will." But I said, "Lord, I will go through if I do." So I asked the Lord to save me. While I was going down into the water, a light came over me, and I was converted. The people saw the change and said that I had fainted. Then began my new life of peace and joy in the Savior's love. I also felt that I had a calling to go out into the highways and byways and gather in the lost sheep.

The church in those days did not believe that women had a right to publicly preach Jesus. Had I told them my heart's desire, they would have mocked me.

Later, I married a Mr. Woodworth. I hoped that now the way would open for me to go out in the work for Jesus. But one trial and hardship after another was my lot. I felt happy with the few little children that God gave us, but soon the Angel of Death took away my bright, blue-eyed, darling boy. One year had hardly passed before another one was taken away.

About this time, my little daughter, Georgia, was converted. We loved so much to talk about the goodness of God and longed for the time when we could meet the little ones over on the other shore. In a short time, she took sick and died. For weeks before she died, her face was all lighted up with the glory of God. She would say, "Oh, Mama, if you could go with me, I would be so happy." I said, "Georgia, I will try." But that would not do. She said, "Oh, Mama, say you will. I cannot die unless you promise to meet me in heaven." I said, "Georgia, by the grace of God, I will meet you in heaven." She said, "Now I am ready. I know you will come."

The Sabbath before she died, she called me to her bedside and said, "Mama, I am going to leave you this week," and she began to set her house in order. She gave her Testament to me. Just before she passed away, she said, "Oh, Mama, I see Jesus and the angels coming for me." It seemed to me that I could see them as they went sweeping through the gates into the New Jerusalem. It was like death to part with my darling, but Jesus was precious to my soul. I could say with David, "They cannot come back to me, but I can go to them." (See 2 Samuel 12:1–23.) Praise the Lord for the Christians' hope.

From the time of the sad occurrences just mentioned, my health was very poor. I seemed to hover between life and death many times. Now I know that all this time God was preparing me for my life's work. I could never dismiss from my mind the call that I had, and Jesus began to give me such wonderful visions. Heaven is a place; its inhabitants are real and not imaginary. I saw Jerusalem in it and talked face to face with Jesus. But I was not willing to go.

When I was alone, I missed my darling so much that I wept as though my heart would break. Then I would always pray; as I prayed, I would forget everything earthly and soar away by faith to the Golden City. There I would see my darlings all together shining in glory and looking at me and saying, "Mama, do not weep for us, but come this way." I would always end by praising and giving glory to God for taking them to such a happy place. Lizzie, our oldest child, aged sixteen, was all we had left of six sweet children.

In all these trials, God was preparing me and opening the way for the great battle against the Enemy of souls; now the great desire of my heart was to work for Jesus. I longed to win a star for the Savior's crown. But when I thought of my weakness, I shrank from the work.

Sometimes when the Spirit of God was striving and calling so plainly, I would yield and say, "Yes, Lord; I will go." The glory of God came upon me like a cloud, and I seemed to be carried away hundreds of miles and set down in a field of wheat where the sheaves were falling all around me. I was filled with zeal and power, and I felt as if I could stand before the whole world and plead with dying sinners. It seemed to me that I must leave all and go at once. Then Satan would *"come in like a flood"* (Isa. 59:19) and say, "You would look nice preaching, being a laughingstock for the people to make sport of. You know you could not do it." I would think of my weakness and say, "No, of course I cannot do it." Then I would be in darkness and despair. I wanted to run away from God, or I wished I could die. But when I began to look at the matter in this way, that God knew all about me and was willing and able to qualify me for the work, I asked Him to qualify me.

I want the reader to understand that at this time, I had a good spiritual experience, a pure heart that was full of the love of God, but I was not qualified for God's work. I knew that I was but a worm. God would have to take a worm to hammer out a mountain. Then I asked God to give me the power He gave the Galilean fishermen—to baptize me for service. I came like a child asking for bread. I looked for it. God did not disappoint me. The power of the Holy Spirit came down as a cloud. It was brighter than the sun. I was covered and wrapped up in it. My body was as light as the air. It seemed that heaven came down. I was baptized with the Holy Spirit and with fire and power, which have never left me. Oh, praise the Lord. There was liquid fire, and the angels were all around in the fire and glory. It is through the Lord Jesus Christ and by this power that I have stood before hundreds of thousands of men and women and proclaimed the unsearchable riches of Christ.

The time finally came when I felt I had to promise God or die. I promised God that if He would restore my health and show me the work, I would do it. I got better immediately. Soon we moved to another settlement, and they took me to church. God seemed to say to me, "I brought you here; go to work." I was very timid. When I rose to testify, I trembled like a leaf; I began to make excuses, saying, "O God, send someone else."

Then the Lord caused me to see the bottomless pit, open in all its horror and woe. There was weeping, wailing, and gnashing of teeth (Matt. 8:12; 13:42). It was surrounded by people who seemed unconscious of their danger and who, without a moment's warning, would tumble into that awful place. I was above them on a narrow plank walk that wound up toward heaven, exhorting and pleading with the people to escape that awful place. This vision left a great impression on my mind. In meetings, when I felt I should talk or pray, I would resist as long as I could; then this awful vision would rise before me, and I would see souls sink into eternal woe. Again I would hear the voice of Jesus whisper, "I am with you; do not be afraid." In a moment, I would be on my feet or knees. I would have been glad to preach if I had been a man and not had so much opposition from my husband and friends.

Several ministers whom I had never seen before told me that God was calling me to the ministry and that I would have to go. Then I thought of going through a course of studies, but I could not get my mind on any study. Everything seemed empty and vacant.

In a vision one night, Jesus asked me what I was doing on the earth. I said, "I am going to work in Your vineyard." He asked, "When?" I answered, "When I get prepared." Jesus said, "Souls are perishing. Go now and tell the people what I have done for you, and I will be with you." I told Him I did not understand the Bible well enough. Then a large open Bible appeared upon the wall, and the verses stood out in raised letters. The glory of God shone around the book. I looked, and I could understand it all. Then Jesus said again, "Go, and I will be with you." I cried, "Lord, where shall I go?" Jesus said, "Go here, go there, wherever souls are perishing."

The first meeting that I undertook to hold was in a little town among my husband's people, where we had lived before. I said, "In the name of the Lord, I will try and leave the results with God." As I rose to speak, this text came to me: *"Set thine house in order: for thou shalt die, and not live"* (Isa. 38:1). The timid spirit left me, and the words came faster than I could give them utterance. People got converted all through the neighborhood.

Soon after this, God led me to a place called the Devil's Den. It was distinguished for infidelity and skepticism. There was an old free church there, in which no one was ever known to be converted. Some of the best ministers had tried to hold meetings there but had left the place in disgust. When I arrived, a large crowd came to see me out of curiosity and expected me to back out. They said, "No one will come." I told them, "If they do not come, I will be alone and pray to God to pour out His Spirit on the people." I also scheduled day meetings.

God came to my rescue. The fire fell. The news spread like fire, and Christians, singers, and ministers came in from miles around. There were hundreds who could not get in the church. An old man and his wife and nine children got converted. Some of the hardest sinners in the whole country got converted. I organized a Sunday school of one hundred and fifty students and appointed a man as superintendent who had been a noted drunkard. From this time forth, "Macedonian calls" (see Acts 16:9) came in constantly, and people would fall like dead men when the power fell. They would lie there for days at a time and have visions and come out brightly converted.

Since the early part of my ministry, which has now been going on for over forty years, some came out of the experience speaking in other tongues. I never felt led to speak much about this experience, but I knew it was of God and that it was according to the Bible. God also gave me the ministry of healing. He showed me that I was to lay hands on the sick and pray for their recovery. The first person that I laid my hands on publicly and prayed for was instantly healed of an incurable disease and turned out to be a wonderful Christian worker in the meeting. This gave me hope and courage. In my ministry I have prayed for hundreds and thousands of people. Almost innumerable people from all walks of life have been healed of all manner of diseases that mankind is susceptible to. Healing for the body, like

The Holy Spirit

salvation for the soul, is in the Atonement and belongs to the Gospel. They should never be separated. I have traveled the continent many times and preached to thousands of people in all the large cities of this country. While always weak in the natural, I followed where the Spirit led and trusted Him for the anointing whenever needed. He has never left me. He bears me up under the anointing and makes me as bold as a lion in bearing witness for my Master. Amen.

For a more complete record of my life, please refer to my book *Signs and Wonders*. *

> Oh, the wonders of creation,
>   And the work of nature's God,
> Call forth songs of admiration
>   As we travel life's rough road.

* See Maria Woodworth-Etter, *Signs and Wonders* (New Kensington, PA: Whitaker House, 1997).

Chapter 1

The Spirit Reveals the Deep Things of God

Eye hath not seen, nor ear heard, neither have entered into the heart of man, the things which God hath prepared for them that love him. But God hath revealed them unto us by his Spirit: for the Spirit searcheth all things, yea, the deep things of God.
—1 Corinthians 2:9–10

This passage is not understood by anyone unless he has the Holy Spirit. Many people today apply this to eternity, to the other world; they think that we never know these things until we get into the other world. I am glad that the Scripture explains itself. *"Eye hath not seen"*—in the natural state. God has, in the present, revealed things to us by His Spirit, by His Spirit in this world. *"The Spirit searcheth all things, yea, the deep things of God."*

I desire to especially call your attention to 1 Corinthians 2:14: *"The natural man receiveth not the things of the Spirit of God: for they are foolishness unto him: neither can he know them, because they are spiritually discerned."*

The natural man cannot understand this wonderful Scripture. There are two classes of men: the spiritual man and the natural man. The natural man is *"poisoned by bitterness and bound by iniquity"* (Acts 8:23 NKJV); the spiritual man is *"born of God"* (1 John 3:9) and walks in the Spirit; he gets out into the deep. The natural man can never discern spiritual things; he can never hear and understand the work of the Lord. These things pass all human understanding. The wisdom of this world, intellect, and science can never understand the spiritual things of God.

There are two kinds of wisdom. *"The wisdom of this world is foolishness with God"* (1 Cor. 3:19). The natural man cannot comprehend the wisdom from above (James 3:17). It never enters his imagination to think of the things God has prepared for those who love Him. He has prepared them already, and He has revealed them to us by His Spirit. His Spirit lets us down into the deep things, even the *"deep things of God."* This is what we preach, what we practice, and what we stand on. The work of the Spirit is foolishness to the natural man; but he who has the Spirit can discern spiritual things.

Various Kinds of Spirits

There are many kinds of power and many spirits going out in the world today. We are told to *"try the spirits"* (1 John 4:1); they are many. Everything is revealed by God through the blessed Holy Spirit. There is only one Spirit that we want anything to do with: not our own spirits, or any other spirit, but the Spirit of the living God. *"As many as are led by the Spirit of God, they are the sons of God"* (Rom. 8:14).

The Spirit will lead us into all truth, all the way. He will lead us where we can get the truth. The child of God will be led into the baptism of the Holy Spirit and of fire (Matt. 3:11), the Pentecostal baptism. Then we can go from one deep thing to another. The Holy Spirit is sent to us by Jesus Christ, and all gifts come through the Holy Spirit. Jesus said of the Spirit, *"'He shall not speak of himself,'* but of Me. He will speak to you and *'show you things to come'* (John 16:13)."* We believe it. Glory to God!

This is the Holy Spirit who came at Pentecost and turned Jerusalem upside down. Jesus said that when the Holy Spirit came, He would abide with us forever (John 14:16), even unto the end. The work of the Spirit is foolishness to the natural man; he cannot comprehend it.

Unless you will hear the voice of God, the voice of the natural man will make you attribute what you see to excitement or to some other power. When the Holy Spirit is poured out, two kinds of people are revealed: one is convinced and convicted, and accepts it; the other says, "If I accept this, I will have to lead a different life and be a laughingstock for the world." They are not willing to pay the price, so they begin to draw back. At first they are amazed at the strange works of God. Then, when they won't accept them, they begin to despise them. Everyone who continues to despise the works of the Holy Spirit will perish.

Counterfeit Power

There are many powers in the world that are not of God but are counterfeit. However, where there is a counterfeit, there is always the genuine. No one ever tries to counterfeit anything that is not genuine; that is a sure evidence that it is genuine.

The Devil shows his power in a good many ways in order to deceive people. He tries to substitute some other power for the power of God. It was so in the time of Moses and the time of the prophets. God's power was especially in the world at certain times, and then magicians would come up with their power and show something that seemed similar. One was of God; the other was of the Devil.

Moses went to Egypt to lead the people out. He threw down his rod before Pharaoh and it became a live serpent. The magicians said they had the same power, so they threw some rods down and they became serpents. One was of God, and the other was of the Devil.

Moses did not get scared and run away. He knew God, and he wouldn't have run if all the serpents in Egypt had come before him. He stood his ground, and I admire him for it; I do not like a coward. What was the result? Moses' serpent swallowed the others up, head and tail! There was nothing left of them. Those who are trying to overthrow the power of God and substitute something else will have a Day of Judgment. The time is coming when the almighty power of God will swallow them up in the *"day of his wrath"* (Rev. 6:17).

The Coming of the Spirit

The Lamb of God left the realm of glory and came down here to be footsore, dusty, weary, and spit upon. He said, *"I come to do thy will, O God"* (Heb. 10:9). If He had not borne all these things, if He had not gone all the way to the cross, the Holy Spirit never could have come. If Jesus had been left in the tomb, the Holy Spirit never could have come. As soon as He arose from the dead and ascended into heaven, the Holy Spirit could come.

God gave His Son the highest place, before all the hosts of heaven. Then He sent the Holy Spirit to dwell in these bodies of ours, His temple (1 Cor. 3:16). The Spirit was to be given after Jesus was glorified. The Holy Spirit is a great power. In the Bible, He is compared to wind, water, and fire.

At Pentecost, He came like a cyclone, a *"rushing mighty wind"* (Acts 2:2). He comes like *"rivers of living water"* (John 7:38). He comes like fire; tongues of fire sat upon each of the disciples at Pentecost (Acts 2:1–4). Wind, water, and fire—the most destructive elements we have, yet the most useful.

God uses these images to denote the mighty power of the Holy Spirit. We see many demonstrations of His mighty power, and *"we cannot but speak the things which we have seen and heard"* (Acts 4:20) of His glory and His majesty. When we know these things, we are witnesses to His power, His majesty, and His glory. Glory to God!

He is a mighty power, and He lives in these bodies of ours. He lets down upon us here an *"eternal weight of glory"* (2 Cor. 4:17), and when we are filled with glory, we have to release it in some way, or we would explode. What are we? We are only worms of the dust. We cannot bear the glory of God; one breath from Him lays us prostrate. In the Bible, we read how men fell when they had a glimpse of God's glory.

Paul tells us that there are those who have a form of godliness but who deny the power thereof; from such we are to turn away (2 Tim. 3:5). *"In the last days perilous times shall come"* (v. 1), and those who have reprobate minds will oppose God's children to their faces, even as the magicians opposed Moses.

In the last days, some people will be living very near to God, but the Devil will have his workers, too, who will attribute signs and wonders to any power except the power of Christ. The Lamb of God, the Lion of the Tribe of Judah, has never lost His power and never will lose His power. I would hate to say by my actions that I thought the Devil had more power than God.

God's Power Is Unlike Any Other

There is a wonderful difference between the power of God and any of those other powers. The Holy Spirit only comes in Christ. He only comes into the bodies of those who love God. When He takes possession of us, He takes us away into the sweetest experience this side of heaven; we are alone with God. He talks to us and reveals to us *"things to come"* (John 16:13).

It is wonderful! God puts us under the power, and God takes us out. No man can bestow this power upon another; it comes only through Jesus Christ. There are two kinds of power, and people who do not know the difference will stand up today and say that wisdom is foolishness.

Many people today have an intellectual faith, a historical faith; they believe. Well, *"the devils also believe, and tremble"* (James 2:19). Belief is one thing; faith is another. *"The letter killeth, but the spirit giveth life"* (2 Cor. 3:6). If the truth is hidden, it is hidden to those who are lost.

The Spirit Reveals the Deep Things of God

Spiritual Manifestations

We may have intellectual imaginations and go through courses of study, learning the doctrines of men. Yet no one but the Holy Spirit can give us a real, abiding, tangible, definite knowledge of the *"things of God."* They seem foolish to the natural man. Sometimes the Holy Spirit gives a spirit of laughter, and sometimes of weeping, and everyone in the place will be affected by the Spirit.

I have stood before thousands of people and been unable to speak; I could only weep. When I was able to see, people were weeping everywhere; that is one way the Holy Spirit works. I have stood for an hour with my hand raised, held by the mighty power of God. When I came to myself and saw the people, their faces were shining.

"God moves in mysterious ways, His wonders to perform." He is the God I worship. Jesus says, "Here am I, and the children You have given me." (See John 17:9–11, 24.) We believe in signs and wonders, not from beneath but from above. We are a people to be wondered at; we are to be a sign among the people.

The heaven of heavens cannot contain God, yet He tabernacles with men. He comes and dwells in us. His gifts are demonstrated through us, so that people may know that God dwells in Zion (Ps. 9:11). We have a bodyguard of angels. The angels of the Lord encamp around those who love God (Ps. 34:7). *"Our citizenship is in heaven"* (Phil. 3:20 NKJV), and we are on the way there.

The Holy Spirit works in many ways. People saw the fire on the disciples' heads at Pentecost. They staggered like drunken men; then the Holy Spirit took possession of their tongues. God Almighty spoke through one hundred and twenty of His children, and they told of His wonderful works. They did not know what they were saying, but every man in that multitude in Jerusalem heard them speak in his own native tongue. (See Acts 2:1–13.)

I am glad God does the same thing today. People who are not saved hate the power of God. The cold, dead formalists cannot understand the power of God; it is foolishness to them. They think people are excited, hypnotized, or have lost their minds.

May God have mercy upon us if we do not know God's power from hypnotic power or the Devil's power! If any man speaks against the Holy Spirit, it will never be forgiven him; to attribute the work of the Holy Spirit to the Devil or to any unclean spirit cannot be forgiven; that is the unpardonable sin. (See Matthew 12:31–32.)

Some people are calling the work of the Holy Spirit the work of the Devil, and they had better beware. There are different kinds of spirits and different kinds of power, and the *"natural man"* (1 Cor. 2:14) cannot understand the work of the Holy Spirit: shining faces, singing, shouting *"as one, to make one sound"* (2 Chron. 5:13), sometimes staggering and falling, *"drunken, but not with wine"* (Isa. 29:9), sometimes speaking *"with other tongues"* (Acts 2:4).

Spiritual Manifestation in Angelic Singing

Praise God, some of the redeemed are getting so filled with the Holy Spirit that He is singing songs through them that none but the redeemed can sing. (See Revelation 14:3.) *"There are diversities of gifts, but the same Spirit"* (1 Cor. 12:4). Paul told us that the Spirit will work in you in one way and in someone else in another way. You know it is the same Spirit who is working, and you do not get jealous when the other person is blessed. No matter how the Spirit works, every member of the body benefits. (See 1 Corinthians 12:1–7.)

People look on these things—they see us lift up holy hands to God, for example—and they don't like it. They are so dead that they cannot get their hands up. Paul said, *"I will therefore that men pray every where, lifting up holy hands"* (1 Tim. 2:8). The psalmist said, *"O clap your hands, all ye people; shout unto God with the voice of triumph"* (Ps. 47:1).

People go to the theater and clap their hands, but when we get our grave clothes off and begin to clap our hands, they think it is an awful thing. David danced with all his might before the ark of the Lord (2 Sam. 6:14), and sometimes the Spirit of God gets into our feet and makes them like *"hinds' feet"* (2 Sam. 22:34).

David said, *"By my God have I leaped over a wall"* (2 Sam. 22:30). How much more will He enable us in these last days, when we are getting ready for a flight in the air! We must get a good supply of this power. The same power that took Jesus up to heaven will take us up one day.

We want more of it, don't we? More of this mighty power. No matter what people say—that it is foolishness, hypnotism, and every other thing—that doesn't make it so. The Spirit will take us out into the deep things, even the *"deep things of God."*

Old Testament Types Revealed in the New

Many things recorded in the Old Testament are types of the work of the Spirit in the New Testament. Many of the movements of God through His children seemed to be foolishness; the messages He gave His prophets to carry seemed very foolish, humanly speaking.

He gave Noah the plans for the ark. There was to be only one window and only one door. Noah built it according to God's plan. He did not heed the jeers of the people, who thought he was losing his mind. He was a laughingstock to everybody; but he went on building, and he proved the wisdom of God in the end.

He built the ark, and God provided the water, more water than they wanted, too much water for them. What happened? God took those who believed Him into the ark and shut the door. The water rose, and the ark went above the treetops—as we are going someday. God is building the ark now, and the works of the Holy Spirit are foolishness to the people who are fighting them.

The ark sailed away, and the world went down, all except Noah and his family. Not many are going into the ark God is building. People are crying, "Foolishness!"

Obedience to God

One time there was a great battle in the land of Israel. The enemy had gathered like consuming grasshoppers. God knew there were a lot of cowards among

His people, and He tested them until only three hundred were left to meet the enemy. God can work by the few as well as the many. He told Gideon what to do; Gideon divided the men into three companies and *"put a trumpet in every man's hand, with empty pitchers, and lamps within the pitchers"* (Judg. 7:16). He said, "When I give the signal, blow the trumpet and say, 'The sword of the LORD, and of Gideon' (v. 18)."

God always has a leader. As they obeyed their leader, something happened. At the signal, they blew the trumpets and broke the pitchers, revealing the lamps. They shouted, *"The sword of the LORD, and of Gideon."*

At the shout and the light, the enemy was frightened to death and started to run, but God sent confusion among them. That little band of three hundred "fanatics" put the whole host of the enemy to flight. What they did seemed foolish, did it not? But what was the outcome? The whole army of the enemy was conquered.

God used a vision—He does sometimes. He told Gideon to go down to the enemy's camp, where Gideon heard a man tell his friend a vision or dream he had had: *"A loaf of barley bread tumbled into the camp of Midian; it came to a tent and struck it so that it fell and overturned, and the tent collapsed"* (Judg. 7:13 NKJV).

His friend interpreted it: *"This is nothing else but the sword of Gideon!...Into his hand God has delivered Midian and the whole camp"* (v. 14 NKJV). So Gideon believed and took courage. (See Judges 6:1–7:23.)

Children of God, those of you who think you are something are really nothing. When you realize you are nothing, God fights for you. How foolish the method of fighting the Midianites seemed! Israel might have said,

"If we break the pitchers, the lamps will show the enemy where we are, and they will shoot us." When God says, "Go forward," obey Him; He takes care of His own.

Truly, God moves in mysterious ways. Remember the fall of Jericho? The city had great walls around it, and all the people of Jericho were shut inside to protect themselves from the Israelites. God told Joshua that he and his men of war should march around the city once a day for six days, with seven priests bearing before the ark of the covenant seven trumpets of rams' horns. On the seventh day, they were to march around the city seven times, with the priests blowing the trumpets. When they made a long blast on the trumpets, the people were to shout, and the walls would fall down. (See Joshua 6:1–20.)

It took faith to do all that marching without any sign of victory and to shout. Why, anyone can shout after the walls fall. Humanly speaking, don't you see how foolish this all was? They had made no preparations for war, only marching and blowing rams' horns. But that was God's way, and they were silly enough to obey God! What was the result? The walls went down.

We could go all through the Word of God in this way. There are so many things that seem so silly, things people would laugh at, but it was God's way, and His servants were willing to obey Him. The result showed God's wonderful wisdom and brought victory through a visible display of His power.

Spiritual Revelation

When these visible signs came, they put a fear of God upon the people; it is the same way with the works of the Holy Spirit. The ways of God and the works of the Spirit are foolishness to the *"natural man"* (1 Cor. 2:14), but what is the outcome?

Paul said, *"If any man among you seemeth to be wise in this world, let him become a fool, that he may be wise"* (1 Cor. 3:18). Later, he said, *"I will [now] come to visions and revelations of the Lord"* (2 Cor. 12:1). He said that he had been carried away to the *"third heaven"*—whether in the body or out of the body, he could not tell (v. 2). He could not tell whether his whole body went or not; he was so light that he could not tell whether he had left his body here or not, but he said, *"God knoweth"* (v. 2). There he heard unutterable things (v. 4).

At another time, Paul was praying in the temple and fell under the power of God; he fell into a trance (Acts 22:17–18). He appeared to be unconscious to the world, but he was never so wide awake to God in his life.

It is during these times that the Spirit of God lets us down into the deep things, even the *"deep things of God."* Peter fell into a trance on the housetop, and God spoke to him three times (Acts 10:9–16). Paul and Silas started out to visit converts. Then Paul had a vision; he saw a man of Macedonia holding out his hands and saying, "Come over and help us." He knew it was the call of God, so they changed their course and went there; this was altogether different from their original plans.

When they began to preach and were arrested, they might have thought they had been mistaken; but Paul knew God, and he never doubted it was God's voice that had called him. They might have said, "If we had not come here, we would have had many people to preach to. Now we have come to this strange place and been put in prison, with our feet fastened in the stocks." The Devil put them in there; but God permitted it, and God delivered them. (See Acts 16:9–10, 16–34.)

There are many wonderful things all around us in these last days, things the natural man cannot understand, demonstrations of God's power. There are other powers, too, and many do not know the difference. God's power is the greatest, and it is the only power that will bring peace to your soul.

God wants you to be pure and holy, filled with the Holy Spirit, but the Devil is right here, too. If you do not know the difference, you will be listening to Satan. He comes sometimes as an *"angel of light"* (2 Cor. 11:14). One word by the Devil in the Garden of Eden upset the world—the little word *"not"* (Gen. 3:4).

When God talks to you, the message agrees with the written Word. The Holy Spirit never says anything that doesn't correspond with the Word. A message that comes from heaven must correspond with the Word; if it is otherwise, do not accept it.

The things of the Spirit that seem foolishness to the world antagonize the Devil, and he sometimes does things that look very similar; but to the one who understands, there is a wonderful difference.

I have been carried away in the Spirit many, many times. Once I was under the power of God for seven hours. I was examined by medical doctors and found to be in a normal condition. Many doctors I know of have been honest enough to say that the power was not hypnotic, even though they could not understand it.

Celebrated Hypnotist Baffled

One of the greatest hypnotists in the world came to our meeting in St. Louis. He had been there two or three days before I knew anything about it. He was surprised to see a man lying there whom hundreds of hypnotists had tried to get under their power; he himself had tried it.

He went to him and tried to bring him out of it, but he could not. After a while, the hypnotist came to me to have an interview. He said he was going to call his friends together and tell them he had found something he could not understand. He could not put anyone under that power or bring anyone out. He said, "If there is a God, I believe this is His power."

When the doctors examined me as I was lying under the power, they said that my pulse was regular, my blood was flowing naturally, and my heart was in a natural condition. I am told that when a person is hypnotized, the blood does not flow naturally. The person is unconscious and simply does what he is told. Someone has to put him in that state and bring him out again.

God does lay His people down under His power, and then He talks to them. I have known people to be a whole week under the power of God. May He seal these truths to our hearts!

I know nothing about hypnotic power, and I have never seen a person hypnotized. But I do know something of the power of God, the power of the Holy Spirit. It is God Himself who sends this power; we can press the button, but God sends the power.

Talk about excitement! This power is the best thing in the world to settle the nerves. These people go down praising God; they continue while they are there, and when they are up, they are still giving God praise.

"Let every thing that hath breath praise the LORD" (Ps. 150:6). People ask why we tell them to praise the Lord. If you do not feel it at first, praise as a *"sacrifice"* (Heb. 13:15), and after a while the praise will come by itself from a soul filled with joy. Hallelujah!

If you will search your Bible, you will find that the things I have told you are true. My words do not amount to anything unless they are backed up by God's Word. The Lord gave me this message, and I have given it to you.

When the power of the Spirit has been so maligned, it is time for you to take a stand for the truth. When a ship is in danger, the sailors come to the front, if they are not cowards. Let us not run away but come to the front.

I stand here in defense of the Gospel. If we are faithful, all things must work together for God's glory (Rom. 8:28). Praise His name.

Chapter 2

"Try the Spirits"

Beloved, believe not every spirit, but try the spirits whether they are of God: because many false prophets are gone out into the world.
—1 John 4:1

There are many spirits that we do not want to have anything to do with. There are our own spirits, the flesh, and the Devil. There are many spirits contending; many times we let our own spirits rule, and we make ourselves think it is God. The same thing happens with the flesh and the Devil.

The Holy Spirit and the Word

Sometimes we know it is not God, but we want to have our own ways. If we have the Holy Spirit, we can prove the spirits, because everything the Holy Spirit does is confirmed by the Word. We do not want to rely on tongues and interpretations alone; we must measure things by the Word. We must measure tongues and demonstrations by the Word, and if they do not agree with the Word, we must not accept them. Everything must be measured by the Word.

We do know God and the voice of God, but the Devil can come as an *"angel of light"* (2 Cor. 11:14). When you are in the Holy Spirit, that is the time the Devil tries to get in and lead you astray. The Holy Spirit is revealing some secret things, and at the same time, the Devil comes in. If you are not careful, you will listen to what he has to say and follow him.

Once I was having a wonderful vision, and right in the midst of it, the Devil said to me, "You are going to die." At the time, I was very sick and had worked myself nearly to death, and I listened to the Devil for a minute. Then I stopped to hear what God wanted to teach me.

I said, "What is this that God is showing me? Does this agree with what God is showing?" I saw there was a big difference. God touched my forehead, the seat of the intellect and reason, and my mouth, signifying courage and power to give forth the message. If I was to give the people His message, I was not going to die; I could not die if I was to do this.

There was someone who attended these meetings whom God was blessing. He wanted to use her, but the Devil came in and made her think that she could do any outrageous thing, and it would be of God.

Do you see how the Devil can lead us astray? She was speaking in tongues and praying, and she said, "Lord, if you want me to kill anyone, I will do it. If you want me to set the camp on fire, I will do it."

That is the way it is with spiritualism. The Holy Spirit never does anything like that. He does not come to kill and knock people's heads off. He deals with them in love and tenderness. People have even offered up children in sacrifice. If you listen to God, the Devil will be put to one side.

These things hurt the Pentecostal movement. God is in it, but the Devil is in it, too. Many people are honest, but they do not understand. God shows them great things that are going to happen, and the Devil comes in and makes them set a specific date for when it will occur.

For some time, Daniel did not understand the vision that he had received. An angel appeared to him to make him understand the vision. (See Daniel 8:1–26.) Be careful that the Devil does not come in and give you another meaning that is altogether different from what God wants you to have.

So many people prophesy this or that, and it never comes true; the prophecy was not according to the Word of God. Someone gives a person a message, and he believes God sent it, but it is not according to the Word.

When God calls you out for His work, He will take care of you. He will give you something to eat and clothe you. There are so many who run before they are sent; it would be better for them not to go at all. Sometimes the Devil uses tongues to upset things generally. Remember that the Devil can speak in tongues, and so can your flesh.

When God speaks in tongues, it means something, and you need to look for the interpretation. God says to ask for the interpretation. Sometimes God gives it through someone else, but we should give the person who speaks in tongues a chance to interpret (1 Cor. 14:13). Be careful that you do not give an interpretation in your own spirit; this hurts the work of God everywhere. Let us *"try the spirits"* and not get in the flesh.

Some people, if they do not like someone, will give a rebuke or a message in tongues and nearly knock the person's head off. This is the work of the Devil. Then someone will get up—some people are so silly—and say, "Don't touch that; it is from the Holy Spirit." They act as if discerning the spirit and motivation of a message were the same thing as "touching God's anointed" or doing harm to a prophet. (See 1 Chronicles 16:22.) Therefore, no one dares to touch it, and the Devil has the whole thing. Then word gets out that the leader of the group sanctions all that, and people do not want to have anything to do with it. The leader may have discernment, but someone will exert pressure on him and say, "Don't touch that." Instead of being so afraid, let us search the Scriptures. God never told anyone to rebuke in an ugly tone.

There was a great work being done in the West. One woman who was in the group said that the United States was going to be destroyed, and that they should go to Japan. They went. People who could not spare the money helped them; they went to escape the destruction.

The whole thing was of the Devil. The United States was not destroyed, they could not speak the Japanese language, they were stranded, and a number of them backslid. They tried to raise money for a great building but never accomplished it. They had been doing a good work here, but deceiving spirits got in.

God gave me a special commission to take the *"precious from the vile"* (Jer. 15:19), and I do not want you to get into the snare of the Devil. So many young people, after their baptism, quit their jobs and start preaching. In a few days, they tell everything they know about the Gospel; then they tell something they don't know. Money to live on does not come in, and many of them backslide.

If God doesn't send you out, don't give up your job; then you will have money to give to God's work. This mistake is made by many missionaries who go abroad. Some sell all they have, break up their homes, and separate from their wives, yet God has not called them.

Gifts and Requirements

The Holy Spirit makes us levelheaded. Remember, those who stayed in the camp got as much as those who went to the battle. (See 1 Samuel 30:1–24.) Be God's stewards, and give the Lord His due. The *"cattle upon a thousand hills"* (Ps. 50:10) are His, but He works through our instrumentality. He gives you everything you have—physically, financially, and spiritually—and He expects you to use all your abilities for Him. If your resources give out, He will supply.

He expects you to take Him into partnership and give Him what belongs to Him, and He will bless you. The Gospel has to be supported. Water is free, but it costs money to lay the pipes and keep the water running. Angels can fly, but men have to pay for transportation; someone has to help with this.

If you keep the pipes in order, the Gospel will be given out. You need to help by praying, by holding up the hands of those who work. (See Exodus 17:12.) If you trust God and walk with Him, that is the work God wants of you.

The Holy Spirit

Don't take up with every vision that comes along. In some places in the Pentecostal movement, people have discarded the Word of God. They don't want a leader, and God always has a leader. When there is none, the Devil takes the chair. God has given some to be pastors and teachers (Eph. 4:11).

Then how does anyone know if God has called him to the ministry? Someone has said that when God calls anyone to do His work, you can hardly get him into the pulpit, but when the Devil calls him, you can't keep him out of it! Those are people who just like to hear themselves talk. Some people want to talk a great deal, bringing in a bone of contention, and it is hurting the work of God everywhere. Leave outside issues alone. God Himself will teach people what to eat, what to wear, and where to go. Many of God's children are fussing about these things. The Lord said that if you do not think it is right to eat meat offered to idols, don't do it, but don't judge another. (See 1 Corinthians 8:1–13.) Therefore, when we open our mouths, let us say something of real spiritual value.

If you have the baptism of the Spirit, you do not need to talk about it; people will know it. Also, let God speak to you. Do not wait for someone to speak in tongues and tell you that God wants you to go to India. Let God speak to you. When people go to a place because someone else has told them that they should go, they get homesick and discouraged and try to get back again. Let the Lord be our Guide. If we do His will, we will know His will.

Lift up Jesus, and try to get people so full of the Holy Spirit that they will live in unity. For example, we do not want to lay hands on anyone suddenly. If we do anything in a spirit of contention, the first thing we know is that everything is in a jumble, and we have done more harm in one meeting than can be imagined.

Lift up Jesus and the Resurrection. Let us *"walk in the light, as he is in the light"* (1 John 1:7). Christ is the great Headlight, and I am earnestly seeking more light than I have ever seen in my life. You have fellowship when you walk in the light (v. 7). We are the lower lights, and He will show us what to do next.

He will say to you, "Now you can do this." You may say, "I did not know before that You would trust me to do this." His answer will be, "You can do it now."

Until God shows you something you're doing wrong, it is not a sin. But after He shows it to you, if you do it, it is a sin. Consecrate everything to God, day by day. He will not call you to do something unless He is going to give you strength and grace.

Having a Teachable Spirit

When you go into a meeting, listen to the teaching. If it does not suit you, and you want something else, the best thing you can do is to go out quietly and drum up a crowd yourself. Some say that you do not need anyone to teach you. (See 1 John 2:27.) It is true that the natural man cannot teach you; however, the spiritual man can teach you.

We know what we are talking about: the spiritual man can teach you. We know nothing as we should, and there is so much for us to know.

As I said earlier, be careful not to lay hands on anyone suddenly. Regarding the recent disturbance here, we profess to be saints, and therefore we want to show forth the Spirit of Christ. We must be firm but kind. Do not speak roughly. The crowds want to be able to see what is going on. Do not speak roughly to the boys. Each one is some mother's boy. When I was young, I would have nearly broken my neck to see what you are seeing.

When they became noisy, it would have been useless to attempt to use force; it would only have ended in a fight, and the plan of the Enemy would have been accomplished. God led me in the only way by which the disturbance could be quelled, and order was restored. God fought for us. God can smite with conviction. The battle is His, not ours.

"Try the spirits." In one of our meetings, there was a black woman who had wonderful spiritual experiences; that is the kind the Devil goes after. One day she commenced to go about on her knees, twisting about like a serpent. God does not tell anyone to do that. She spoke in tongues; then she said, "I don't want to do it; I don't want to do it."

Everyone knew it was not of God, and I said to her, "That is not God. The Enemy has gotten hold of you." At first, she didn't want to give it up; but the next day God showed her, and she asked to be delivered. The Devil had gotten in and caused her to do things that were not right, in order to kill her influence.

Spiritual versus Spiritualism

A woman came to me and said, "I am afraid that this spirit that is upon me is not of God. I was baptized in the Holy Spirit. I went into a mission where they did everything by tongues, and they got me so mixed up, I did not know where I was. Then, this spirit got hold of me; it shakes my head and makes my head ache."

That is spiritualism. For two years, this woman could not give a testimony. But God rebuked the shaking spirit, the power of God came into her hands and voice, and she gave a testimony for God.

Some people, when they pray for and lay hands on a person, throw the slime off. Again, that is spiritualism. Don't ever do anything like that. When you lay hands on a person, God takes care of the evil spirit. If you are filled with the Holy Spirit, the Devil is outside you; keep him out. Be careful who lays hands on you, for the Devil is counterfeiting God's work.

That is what ails the Pentecostal movement; so much of this has crept in. Some people take every foolish thing as if it is from the Holy Spirit. There are two extremes: some Christians prevent the Holy Spirit from working except in a certain way. Others think everything is of the Holy Spirit. They say, "Don't touch it; it is of God." One is as bad as the other. Let everything be done by the Word of God.

We are living in the last days, and there has got to be a higher standard for the Pentecostal movement. Christ is coming, and we cannot continue in the old rut. God is sifting us today, and we have to rise above errors; we have to rise up and go forward. By the grace of God, we will. Praise His name!

Chapter 3

The Unpardonable Sin

D ear friends, we have met in the presence of the Most High God; we have come to do business for Jehovah. Let us do it well. We will meet again in eternity. Let us be very solemn. God's reporter is taking note of every thought, every action here tonight, of those who are against Him and those who are for Him. So let us turn our minds from the fleeting things of life, the things that are passing away, and be shut in with God this hour.

The message the Lord has brought before us is found in Matthew 12:31–32:

> *Wherefore I say unto you, All manner of sin and blasphemy shall be forgiven unto men: but the blasphemy against the Holy Ghost shall not be forgiven unto men. And whosoever speaketh a word against the Son of man, it shall be forgiven him: but whosoever speaketh against the Holy Ghost, it shall not be forgiven him, neither in this world, neither in the world to come.*

The Holy Spirit

This message comes to us from Jesus, as much as if He were standing here. Hear the eternal Word from the lips of the Son of God now reigning in glory. The words are just as powerful today as when they came from His lips, if they go forth by the power of the Holy Spirit.

This subject is considered one of the deepest in the Word of God. You have often heard the question asked, "What is the unpardonable sin?" And some people are very much concerned about having committed it. John says, *"There is a sin unto death: I do not say that* [you] *shall pray for it"* (1 John 5:16); but other sins are not unto death (v. 16), and through prayer God will wash them all out.

The Danger of Blasphemy

Blasphemy against God and all kinds of sin against Him and against mankind will be blotted out, but whoever speaks against the Holy Spirit has no forgiveness, either in this world or in the world to come. Christ made this statement because the Pharisees said He had an evil spirit and did His mighty works through that agency. So, you see, it is an unpardonable sin to attribute any of the mighty works of the Holy Spirit to the Devil. Since the early church, there has never been a time when there was so much danger of people committing the unpardonable sin as there is today. This is because the Pentecostal fire has encircled the earth, and tens of thousands have received the Holy Spirit, feeling His presence. This has been backed up by signs and wonders and diverse operations of the Spirit.

When men and women come in contact with this work of the Holy Spirit, hearing His words and seeing

His works, there is danger lest they attribute the power present to an agency other than the Spirit of God, lest they condemn the power and condemn God's servants. How often have we heard ministers say, when they heard men and women and children speaking in other tongues, "Oh, it is the work of the Devil." Now you hear what God says about it; they are speaking against the Holy Spirit. God has been working in this city and is going to work in much greater measure. We expect to see greater signs and wonders. If the saints stand together as one, pray together, and shout victory, God will show Himself as a mighty God and a Savior.

The Spirit Comes in Many Ways

God will not only come in healing power, but will manifest Himself in many mighty ways. On the Day of Pentecost, Peter said, "[Jesus] *hath shed forth this, which ye now see and hear*" (Acts 2:33). And from what they saw and heard, three thousand acknowledged that it was the power of God and turned to Christ. Others stifled conviction and turned away, saying, "This is the work of the Devil." When the Holy Spirit is poured out, it is either *"life unto life"* or *"death unto death"* (2 Cor. 2:16). It is *"life unto life"* to those who go forward and *"death unto death"* to those who blaspheme against the Holy Spirit. So we want to be careful what we say against the diverse operations, supernatural signs, and workings of the Holy Spirit. Some people look on and say, "It looks like hypnotism" or "I believe they are mesmerized." To others, it appears to be mere foolishness, even as the Scripture says of the *"natural man"*: *"the things of the Spirit of God…are foolishness unto him…because they are spiritually discerned"* (1 Cor. 2:14).

The Holy Spirit

It was the same on the Day of Pentecost, when a multitude saw the disciples staggering about under the power of the Spirit, speaking in tongues. While some said, "They are drunk" (see Acts 2:13), others knew that the mighty power of God was there.

There is a power here that is not of earth, a power lifting people up, making men and women upright, making them good neighbors, good husbands and wives. It is the mighty presence of Almighty God. Observe the lives of these people. They do not seek worldly amusements, but the power of God is manifested in them.

What did the power bring on the Day of Pentecost? The people who came together were all amazed and said, "We never saw anything like this before." Everybody began to get convicted, though some, who were not willing to accept it, not willing to be called fools for Christ's sake, rejected it. To ease their guilty consciences, they said, "They are drunk."

They knew better. They knew that the mighty power of God was there; if there was a question about it, God settled it. Peter got up in the midst of them and said, "These men are not drunk, as you say. Men don't get drunk at nine o'clock in the morning. Rather, this is what was spoken by Joel the prophet: *'In the last days, saith God, I will pour out of my Spirit upon all flesh: and your sons and your daughters shall prophesy, and your young men shall see visions, and your old men shall dream dreams'* (Acts 2:17). This is the Holy Spirit that you now see and hear." (See Acts 2:15–17, 33.)

It is the same Holy Spirit today. The Holy Spirit is the Spirit of God. He is a person, and He works under the direction of Jesus Christ, under His orders.

He doesn't do anything except what Christ tells Him to do. When we are ready to receive Him, Jesus sends the Holy Spirit to impart to us His own gifts. The Holy Spirit cleanses these temples of ours and comes in to dwell. He fills our bodies, and His power in us gives us utterances in tongues (see Acts 2:4) and works through us in other ways.

The Mission of the Holy Spirit

Now, in order to guard against committing the unpardonable sin, we must know a little of what the Holy Spirit is. He could not come until Christ was glorified. Christ was on the earth in His human body for only a short time, but at Pentecost, He came to stay through the Holy Spirit.

Jesus said that when the Holy Spirit comes, *"whom the Father will send in my name"* (John 14:26), He will abide with us forever (v. 16). And He will not speak on His own; rather, He will say what He hears (16:13).

I love the Holy Spirit because He is always witnessing for Jesus, and He comes to bring us power (Acts 1:8). He is *"the Comforter...the Spirit of truth"* (John 15:26) who will abide forever (14:16). He brings all things to our remembrances (14:26). We are so forgetful in our natural state. But we have spiritual minds, and God writes His Word on our minds and on the tablets of our hearts (Heb. 10:16). The Holy Spirit brings these messages to us at the right time—a message to this one who is in sin, that one who is in sorrow—messages from heaven that encourage the weak and help the strong and always point us to Jesus, the great Burden-Bearer.

The Holy Spirit

"Rivers of living water" (John 7:38) flow from us through the Holy Spirit, and healing power goes out. Power went out from Peter, so that the sick whom his mere shadow fell upon were healed (Acts 5:14–16). Power went out from Paul, so that handkerchiefs and aprons that he had touched were taken to the sick, and when they were laid on the afflicted, streams of healing went forth and devils were driven out (Acts 19:11–12).

The Holy Spirit is called *"water"*: *"I will pour water upon him that is thirsty, and floods upon the dry ground: I will pour my spirit upon thy seed, and my blessing upon thine offspring"* (Isa. 44:3). A tidal wave of glory is coming this way. May God help us to be as empty vessels, so that the Holy Spirit's power may fill us to overflowing. In addition to *"water,"* the Holy Spirit is spoken of in the Bible as *"fire"* (Matt. 3:11) and *"wind"* (Acts 2:2)—three of the most destructive elements in the world, and three of the most useful. We could not live without fire, wind, or water.

Mighty Winds and Heavenly Zephyrs

When a cyclone comes, men and women turn pale. When God's cyclone through the Holy Spirit strikes the people, it is a great leveler. They lose sight of their money bags, and all hatred and ill will are swept away, just as a cyclone carries away everything before it. When a tidal wave strikes a city, it submerges everything. In the same way, in a tidal wave of the Holy Spirit, everything goes under. Oh, we need a cyclone of God's power to sweep out of our lives everything that hinders us and a tidal wave to submerge us in God.

The Unpardonable Sin

God uses these great elements, fire, wind, and water, in all their force to give us an idea of the mighty power of the Holy Spirit. Our bodies are His temples. As great pieces of machinery are moved by electricity, so our bodies, the most wonderful pieces of machinery ever known, are moved by the power of the Holy Spirit *"sent down from heaven"* (1 Pet. 1:12). On the Day of Pentecost, the Spirit filled the one hundred and twenty disciples with power to witness for Jesus. At the hands of the apostles, God healed the sick, and He heals today by the same power. God pours out *"rivers of living water"* (John 7:38). Therefore, what manner of people ought we to be?

If we don't have the power, let us confess it and ask God to give us the power He gave the first disciples. If those who come to the Lord will be filled as the disciples were on the Day of Pentecost, we will have streams of living water rushing through us and flowing to the very ends of the earth. Jesus Christ was baptized in the Holy Spirit, but He did not have *"all power"* (Matt. 28:18) until He had finished His course. He could have turned away and not gone to the cross, but He went all the way and cried, *"It is finished"* (John 19:30). His last act was this going down into death.

But God Almighty raised Him up, and when He was resurrected, *"all power"* was given to Him (Matt. 28:18)—all power! He sent His disciples out in His name and said that those who believed in Him would cast out devils, speak in new tongues, and heal the sick by the laying on of hands; if they drank anything deadly (accidentally, of course), it would not hurt them (Mark 16:17–18). He said to the disciples, "Do not marvel at what you see. You will do these things if you believe, and *'greater works than these shall* [you] *do; because I go unto my Father'* (John 14:12)."

The Holy Spirit

The Pentecost Shower Falls

Now, when Pentecost came, the disciples were in the Upper Room, waiting. They were all saved and pure and of one accord—there were no divisions and there was no controversy (Acts 1:13–14). They did not know how the *"promise of the Father"* (v. 4) was going to come, but they were waiting for it. Suddenly, the Spirit came like a cyclone and filled the whole building; a great tidal wave of power was turned upon them, and they were all filled with *"living water"* (John 7:38). The Spirit's tongues of fire were upon their heads (Acts 2:2–3), and they all began to speak in other tongues as the *"Spirit gave them utterance"* (v. 4).

The people who came running up were amazed and said, "What does this mean? Are not all these Galileans who are speaking? Are they not ignorant of these foreign tongues? Yet everyone hears them speak in his own native language!" (See Acts 2:7–8.) It was the Holy Spirit who gave them these utterances in other languages. The Lord had said, *"'With stammering lips and another tongue will* [I] *speak to this people,'* but for all that, they will not believe" (Isa. 28:11–12). He emphasized that, and the people heard and knew it; yet in spite of all that, they mocked and cried out that the men had been drinking.

Peter Preaches in the Power of the Spirit

The Holy Spirit came to testify of Jesus. The Spirit preached the first sermon on Jesus' resurrection through Peter, who got up and brought forth the Scriptures to prove that this manifestation was of the Holy Spirit and that the Spirit witnessed of Christ.

The Unpardonable Sin

People who had not believed that Jesus was the Christ—though He did works that no one else did (John 15:24) and spoke as no man had ever spoken (7:46)—were now brought under conviction, and three thousand souls were converted on that day. When they saw the operations of the Holy Spirit, many in Jerusalem believed, *"and a great company of the priests were obedient to the faith"* (Acts 6:7).

The Holy Spirit is here today bringing Jesus into our midst. He is healing the sick by the power of God; devils are being cast out, and miracles are being worked in the mighty name of Jesus through the power of the Holy Spirit. God is giving visions. Proverbs 29:18 says, *"Where there is no vision, the people perish."* People are having visions today of the Second Coming of the Lord, of the Marriage Supper of the Lamb, and of the Rapture.

The Holy Spirit comes with weeping. He makes you weep because of what is coming on the earth. Oh, there are signs of trouble! The unbelieving world is going to be cast out into darkness; but while we sigh and weep at the sad condition of the world (see Ezekiel 9:4), we rejoice to know that Jesus is coming soon.

Prophecy Comes True

We were holding meetings in Moline, Illinois. One night an evangelist came in whom we had never seen before. We were talking about the baptism of the Holy Spirit, which she had heard about and was hungry for. I said to her, "You are going to get the baptism tonight." Well, there was not much sign of it happening as I got up to give the Word. She sat in front of me, and while I was talking, she looked as if she were asleep; however, the power of God was upon her. The Word was going out, and the lightning struck. When I finished talking, the power was on her in a wonderful way, and she commenced speaking in tongues and interpreting.

Then she wailed the saddest wail I ever heard. It struck me that it was like the daughters of Jerusalem weeping over the destruction of the temple. (See Luke 23:28–31.) It was so painful, so doleful, that everyone was made sad. I said, "This is the signal of some great sorrow, distress, anguish, and trouble that is coming on the people." God showed me that it was a signal of distress, of awful calamity that was coming. At the same time, a sister said that she saw a great earthquake and described how the water swept over the corpses and down the street. The next day in the newspapers, there was an account of the dreadful destruction by earthquake that had occurred in Kingston, Jamaica.

Do you not see the hand of God in that vision? It was something that, coming true immediately, would convince the people. In Dallas last year, the Lord showed us many things that took place in Turkey when the armies came together. An old brother in Dallas had visions of the battles before they took place, and he saw multitudes being killed.

The Spirit Gives Heavenly Music

The Holy Spirit brings gifts, miracles, and the discerning of spirits. We laugh and cry in the Spirit; we shout and dance and leap; our bodies get so light we scarcely touch the earth.

The Unpardonable Sin

At our last meeting in Long Hill, Connecticut, the heavenly choir surpassed anything I have ever heard before. We had it two or three times a day, and there wasn't any discord. It was the Holy Spirit making harmony through these believers, and the singing was not earthly singing, but heavenly. Sometimes I would be a little late in getting to the meeting, and as I came up the hill, the sound of the heavenly choir wafted down. It sounded as if it came from heaven; it was the song of the redeemed.

A Song Only the Redeemed Can Sing

God is getting His children ready to sing at the Marriage Supper of the Lamb. They sing a song no one can sing except the redeemed. (See Revelation 14:3.) No outsiders can join them. The Spirit has shown me that the coming of the Lord is very near, and I know it now more than ever.

God baptized me over twenty-five years ago with a wonderful baptism, but I am more spiritually hungry today than I ever was. I see greater possibilities today than ever before.

Let us advance from one degree of glory to another. (See 2 Corinthians 3:18.) Blessed is the servant who, when his master comes, is found at his post, giving to the household their portion of *"meat in due season"* (Matthew 24:45–46). This is your opportunity, your day of God's visitation. The bride has *"made herself ready"* (Rev. 19:7). You cannot go to the tailor and order your suit for the banquet; you have to make it yourself. The bride has made herself ready, and it is going to be the most wonderful wedding garment you ever heard of.

It takes skill to weave the garment of pure linen and to embroider the finely made linen work. (See Psalm 45:14.) When the bride is ready, the Bridegroom will greatly admire her. There will be a great company of guests in the banquet hall. But some of us are not ready; we do not have our garments. The time has come to get ready. Oh, it means something to dress for the Marriage Supper of the Lamb. When there is a banquet in honor of a king's son or daughter, it is a great occasion, and the musicians are trained for it long beforehand. Now, this Banquet that is going to take place in the skies, this Marriage Supper of the Lamb, will be the greatest wedding ever known.

The King's Bride

The King of Glory will be married to His bride. Don't you know that every good thing the world enjoys, God is going to let us enjoy ten-thousandfold? When we eat bread and drink wine in the kingdom (see Matthew 26:29; Luke 22:30), it will be the greatest Banquet, the most wonderful occasion ever heard of.

The bride is now in training. The Holy Spirit is the Dove; the singing is the cooing of the Dove before the storm. Have you ever heard doves, before a storm, calling to their mates to seek shelter? In a similar way, the Holy Spirit is calling to us to seek shelter from the Tribulation storms that are coming upon the earth.

The Lord has us in training. He is making our bodies light and supple so that we can go up to meet Him in the air. May the Lord help us to be filled with the Holy Spirit so that we can rise. The Spirit is the only moving power in the church of Christ, the mighty

The Unpardonable Sin

Agent. He was sent to continue the ministry of Jesus through the body of Christ.

Let us get the fire from heaven that will enable us to do business for God, and let us be careful that we do not attribute the power of God to the Devil, lest this leads to the unpardonable sin.

Chapter 4

Christ's Great Revival
on the Plains

*And it came to pass in those days, that he went out
into a mountain to pray, and continued all night in
prayer to God. And when it was day, he called unto
him his disciples: and of them he chose twelve, whom
also he named apostles....And he came down with
them, and stood in the plain, and the company of
his disciples, and a great multitude of people out of
all Judaea and Jerusalem, and from the sea coast of
Tyre and Sidon, which came to hear him, and to be
healed of their diseases; and they that were vexed
with unclean spirits: and they were healed. And the
whole multitude sought to touch him: for there went
virtue out of him, and healed them all.*
—Luke 6:12–13, 17–19

This was one of the greatest revivals that Jesus
Christ ever held. There were great and wonderful results. We find much preceding these verses:

the Son of God had healed a lame man who had a withered arm (Luke 6:6–10), the Devil had stirred up the Pharisees, and they began to plot how they might kill the Son of God (v. 11). However, He slipped away from the crowd and went into the mountains and prayed all night alone with God. If the Son of God found it necessary to pray all night alone with God, don't you think we ought to spend some time alone with God?

He was probably fasting. When Jesus Christ fasted, something happened afterward. If God puts a fast upon you, and you do as He directs, something will happen afterward—and it will not be that your body is afflicted and that you are all out of sorts and making everybody miserable around you when you are finished. That is not God's fast. When Jesus went out and fasted and prayed, some great miracle always took place afterward.

When Jesus received His baptism at the Jordan, the Holy Spirit came upon Him to stay, and He was led into the wilderness. He was alone with God for forty days, fasting all that time, and was among the wild beasts (Mark 1:12–13). After the forty days, the fasting and praying were over, and He was hungry. He was not hungry all the time He was fasting; however, we are told that afterward, He was hungry.

The Devil is always at hand, so the Devil tempted Him in an amazing way by asking Him to make bread out of stones. Of course, He could have done it, but you see, while He was fasting with God and communing with the Spirit, He got power to counter the Devil. The Devil came with all his force. But Jesus had won the victory in prayer while He was alone with God, and He was enabled to drive the Devil back. (See Matthew 4:1–11.)

Another time, after He had been alone in the mountains praying, a great storm came. The disciples thought the ship was about to go down, but He calmed the tempest and the sea became as glass. (See Matthew 14:23–32.)

In our Scripture text, He was alone with God all night in prayer on the mountain. He was not talking to the wind; He was talking with His Father, the God of heaven. He was about to undertake something requiring great wisdom and mighty power from God. He was about to select the pillars that were going to establish the church of Christ—the church of the living God.

Jesus Christ could not be hidden, and if you are filled with God as you ought to be, you cannot be hidden, either. He could not be hidden, and when He came out of His hiding place, He saw the disciples and a great multitude who were watching and waiting for Him. He called the disciples together to do a mighty work. He had many thousands following Him who had been healed and wonderfully blessed and who knew a great deal about the Son of God, so He had a mighty responsibility to choose the right apostles.

He selected twelve and ordained them. He clothed them with power. He gave them license from heaven— God-given authority. He filled them with the Holy Spirit. He loaned them the same power that He had over all devils and unclean spirits. He told them to go out two by two and preach the same Gospel He was preaching, in the same way. He told them to exercise the same faith He had exercised with God—to cast out devils and heal the sick. He qualified them and ordained them with power from on high to go forth to

The Holy Spirit

accomplish the same results that He had accomplished. This was wonderful.

We read that Jesus and all the disciples went down from the mountain into the plains. We are told that great multitudes followed Him from Judea—a multitude is not less than five hundred people—and multitudes came out of all Judea and Jerusalem, from the seacoast of Tyre and Sidon, and out of towns all along the seacoast and from every direction.

There must have been many thousands out there in the hot sun. What did they come for? They came to hear Jesus, not just to get healed, like some of you. They came to hear about Jesus, to get acquainted with Him, to see Him whom to know is *"life eternal"* (John 17:3). They came to hear the Word that He brought from heaven, to find out the way that they might be saved and healed. They had a wonderful meeting there.

Remember, they came to hear the Word and to see. *"Faith cometh by hearing"*—hearing the Word of God (Rom. 10:17). How can they hear the Word of God without a preacher, and how can he preach the Word of God unless God has sent him (vv. 14–15)? How are people to get faith for healing today when you preach against it? How will they get faith about the coming of the Son of God when you don't talk about it? Faith comes by hearing the Word of God. No man can get down into the mysteries of God without the enlightening power of the Holy Spirit. If the Bible is sealed, it is sealed to those who are lost, who are blinded by the *"god of this world"* (2 Cor. 4:4). But this glorious Gospel brings you into communication with Jesus, God Almighty's dear Son, and with the Father who sent Him.

A Divine Healing Meeting

So these people were gathered there to hear and get acquainted with Jesus and to find the way to be healed. The first thing Jesus did after ordaining the disciples for the ministry was to take them into the greatest revival He ever held and give them a start for the great work they had to do. It was a divine healing meeting from start to finish. Jesus Christ preached the Glad Tidings—salvation for the soul and healing and redemption for the body. He preached the double cure; otherwise, His fame never would have gone out over that country. They heard about the Great Physician, about His mighty love and power. No case was too hard for Him. No one was too poor or too rich, if they came in God's way. He healed everyone, and He not only healed but He also saved them, for He gave them the double cure. He Himself took our infirmities and bore our sicknesses, and by His stripes we are healed today (Isa. 53:5).

"Which is easier, to say, 'Your sins are forgiven you,' or to say, 'Rise up and walk'?" (Luke 5:23 NKJV). One is as easy as the other. Both are miracles, God's power being demonstrated. The same power saves the soul and heals the body, and it will take us up to glory. It will make us so light that we will rise without wings. Hallelujah!

So the Lord preached the Word to these people, and they were healed, every one. *"'Man, thy sins are forgiven thee'* (Luke 5:20). *'Behold, thou art made whole: sin no more, lest a worse thing come unto thee'* (John 5:14). Go and tell your friends, every one, what great things the Lord has done. Don't forget it. Don't be so forgetful of His benefits. Serve God, give glory to God, and that disease will never come back. Go—you are whole. Go,

and sin no more, lest it come back and you die or something worse comes." Glory to God. You must see how
much glory God is to get out of this. Hallelujah! When
He healed the body, He saved the soul.

All kinds of people gathered in the plains came
out to see Jesus. Did you come here to see Jesus, or did
you come here out of curiosity? I hope that if you came
through curiosity, you are satisfied by this time. They
came to see Jesus, to get acquainted with Him and to
hear the blessed doctrine He was preaching. They came
to learn the way to God and to get this great salvation.
It cost such a terrible price, but God is offering it to
you *"without money and without price"* (Isa. 55:1). Glory to
God. Accept it.

Shocks from the Heavenly Battery

These disciples were initiated in a great revival.
Jesus preached as no man had ever preached. (See John
7:46.) He preached the Glad Tidings: salvation from sin
and healing from their diseases. He preached the Word
and made it plain. He gave them to understand that
"whosoever will" may come (Rev. 22:17). Oh, you nervous
people, you who are going to have an operation, God
can keep you from all these things. *"I am…the God of
all flesh"* (Jer. 32:27). Is there anything too hard for
Jesus? (See verse 27.) No. He can move the mountain
of tumor in a minute. He can remove the cancer and
soothe your nerves. You who are afraid that the excitement will make you nervous: get a shock from the bat-
tery of heaven, and you will sleep like a baby. He is the
very same Jesus, the wonder-working Jesus, *"the same
yesterday, today, and forever"* (Heb. 13:8 NKJV). Glory! I am
a witness.

Jesus went out to preach, and He did not have a lot of music to accompany Him. There were no pianos, but the power of God was there. It is not so much music, singing, long prayers, or preaching that is effective, but the Spirit of the living God. When Jesus opened His mouth, He spoke as no man had ever spoken (John 7:46), because there was something behind it. His Word was like the hammer that breaks the hard rock, like coals of fire on the mind. It lodged in the heart; it was like arrows dipped in the blood of Jesus, shot out by the lightning of God's power to strike men in the forehead, causing them to fall like dead men.

Go to the Cross

Move out of the city of destruction; move to the cross. Get out of the plains, and start for glory. They had a wonderful meeting there. Jesus preached the Word. He showed them it was for them. He showed them how to come. He showed them what they had to do, and they met the conditions. Every last one of them had to believe in Jesus and get close enough to touch Him.

Someone touched me. Glory! How do I know? I felt the power going out. (See Mark 5:25–34.) If you touch Jesus Christ with faith, God will come, even if He has to bring heaven down. It isn't the long prayer or the flowery prayer that is effective, but the prayer of faith—faith that touches God and brings heaven down. Hallelujah!

The preaching was over; the altar call was given; they began to make their way to Jesus, and they stood on the watch. Faith comes by watching. Faith came to them as they heard and saw the wonderful testimonies

The Holy Spirit

that were occurring right in front of them. We see them trying to come, trying to get there first. Everyone who came received. If they had faith, it did not take two or three hours for the flash of light to come from heaven.

These people accepted it. They did not carry their sick back over those plains in the hot sun. Rather, they touched Him, and the result was that the diseases left and the demons went out like dogs. The healing power of Jesus went in, and their bodies were healed. Then they went out to bring in others. Is that what you are doing? Or are you sitting down and waiting for the power to come back? Bless the Lord.

So their faith grew into knowledge. When they first came, they saw and heard, but now they knew it was so. They saw it before their eyes. They saw people running, leaping, and skipping in every direction. The "excitement," as many call it today, ran high, and everyone got in the battle. When you begin to get your eyes on Jesus Christ, you can tell it. So their faith grew, and pretty soon the multitudes decided they would all just rush forward. Then the whole congregation—thousands of people—made a rush to try to touch the Son of God, and everyone who touched Him was made whole.

He cast out devils, saying, "You deaf spirit, you dumb spirit, come out." Jesus Christ came to destroy the works of the Devil. So the multitude tried to touch Him, and everyone got the double cure: salvation for the soul and body. They got joy in their hearts. Do you believe it? Praise the Lord!

So this was a great revival. Jesus cast out the demons. Those possessed with demons will do all kinds of foolish, devilish things to torment everyone. But when Jesus came, the demons knew they had to leave.

It is the same way today. The demons will have to leave if you come into the truth. Christ has given you authority and power to cast out devils in His name. The devils will run like dogs. *"Resist the devil, and he will flee from you"* (James 4:7). But you have to keep the devils out, or they will try to get in again. (See Luke 11:24–26.) You keep them out.

The demoniac in Luke 8:26–33 represents tribulation. The man had had these devils all his life. But Jesus said, "You come out of him, and don't you ever go in anymore." He will cast the devils out of you, but you have to keep them out yourself. If you get your house full of the glory of God and give the Lord the key, you will not be bothered anymore.

The Double Cure

This was a glorious revival, and Jesus initiated His disciples into ministry there to give them courage. They went out with gladness, filled with the Spirit of mighty power. They went into the villages and cities and preached the Gospel—the double cure (Luke 9:1–6, 10). They had never heard it before, but they preached the Gospel and healed the sick everywhere. Wherever they preached the double cure, somebody believed and was healed. If they had not preached it, no one would have known anything about it. Glory to God! You find this all through the Word of God. Some of the greatest work that Jesus ever did was healing the sick and casting out devils.

We are told that Jesus Christ was anointed by God and began to preach and heal the sick of all kinds of diseases, *"for God was with him"* (Acts 10:38). He was anointed by God to do this. Preach the Gospel, and demonstrate and prove it to be from God by healing the sick. Wherever Jesus went, He did that. The greatest revivals in the New Testament after Pentecost were the direct result of people witnessing one or more divine healings of the body.

The incidences of healing in the Word of God show us that healing is the most effective way in which people are drawn to Christ. Nearly all of the great revivals were brought about by divine healing, and sometimes only one was healed. The man at the Beautiful Gate was healed and got the double cure. Peter and John were just going in to the temple to preach. The result was that five thousand men were converted that day, and Peter and John were thrown into prison. (See Acts 3:1–4:4.) If you are all right, you are going to be persecuted. But Peter and John began to shout and rejoice; they had results and were willing to sit in prison when they thought of the souls that had been saved. Hallelujah!

Hundreds have been healed here. Look how hard your hearts are! You would not believe God if He walked across the platform. May God sweep away this damning sin of unbelief. We find that Jesus gave to His disciples the same power that He had. He ordained seventy and sent them out. He first chose twelve, and a few days later, He chose seventy and gave them power over all kinds of devils. They went out and had great success. As soon as they believed Jesus Christ, they had power. (See Luke 10:1–20.)

The Word was demonstrated by signs and wonders following (Mark 16:17–18), and so God's Word must be demonstrated today. All through the Word, from Genesis to Revelation, whenever God gave a message to one or two—the message looked very foolish from a human standpoint; it took wonderful faith to go out and carry the message, but they knew God—whenever they went out and carried a message in God's way, something happened. The Lord God came in a visible way with signs from heaven that all the people could see. God demonstrated that message. So these visible signs of the Spirit are the Word demonstrated.

Demons of Witchcraft and Sorcery

The working of God's Spirit is foolishness to man (1 Cor. 2:14). You go to some hypnotist or spiritualist and let him call up the dead, and he can pull the wool over your eyes; yet you would rather believe that than believe Jesus Christ. Satan's workers always try to counterfeit the real, don't they? God works today, and the Devil works. In Bible times, there were witches and sorcerers, but God's people knew Him, and all through the Old Testament, God demonstrated His Word. The Israelites acted like crazy people, but God was with them. He always came to the rescue, and those who laugh last, laugh best. The result of Jesus' disciples going out preaching the Gospel and healing the sick was that the fire of God fell on the people. They thought these men must be connected with heaven.

So the working of the Holy Spirit is foolishness to the natural mind. The Holy Spirit is not discerned by the natural man. But if you go to God and get the oil of heaven, you will have light on the blessed Word of God. God will talk to your heart, and Christ will be real, salvation will be real, and heaven will be real because the Spirit of God will let you down into the *deep things of God*" (1 Cor. 2:10). Glory to God!

The Holy Spirit

It was so on the Day of Pentecost when the Holy Spirit came. Some said that the disciples were drunk. (See Acts 2:1–13.) They lied about the Holy Spirit, and people have been lying about Him ever since, but the work went on just the same. Glory to God! People have always persecuted the work of God, grieved the Holy Spirit, and treated the blood of Christ as something unholy.

If you don't know, if you don't believe, if you don't understand, ask God about these things. Don't go to some old infidel. Go to God. You say, as they did then, "What do you think of it? Have any of the scribes believed?" This is what they said before: "Have any of our smart men believed yet?"

You better believe in Christ and seek the wisdom that comes from above. (See James 3:17.) He will make you wise in spiritual things. They are foolishness in the sight of man; however, the wisdom of God, the things of God, are eternal, and they are what will take us to heaven. I praise God for this wonderful salvation.

Now I want to say a few more words concerning the work I know about. I have been standing before the public for forty years, and God has given me grace and courage to stand. I have preached the Gospel in nearly every denomination. Thousands have gone out as ministers and workers. Many saints have gone home to glory.

We have been praying for the sick. If you have read my book *Signs and Wonders*, you will remember that when I started out, I did not know I would have to pray for the sick; but I was sick myself, and God healed me and raised me from my deathbed. My friends said, "Somehow, I believe God is going to raise you up." I did not look like it, but I knew inside that God wanted me to do something. I promised God that if He would raise me up and show me His way, I would do it.

I started out after God baptized me in the Holy Spirit. I knew God was calling me for public service. I knew I would die unless God came to me like He did to the fishermen. I told the Lord that if He would baptize me with power and knowledge, I would undertake the work. I would go to the ends of the earth and live a thousand years, if I might take one soul to heaven. So the Lord wonderfully baptized me and sent me out. I did not try to heal then—I don't now; God does the healing. But after a while, God showed me I must pray for the sick. I had a big battle; I nearly lost my soul before I would consent. He had to give me power. Bless God, He did.

After that, I began to pray for the sick. When God comes, the Devil comes. I was holding meetings in a big skating rink. The Devil kept telling me, "Oh, if you start praying for the sick, they will bring wagonloads of people. Nobody will be saved, and your original purpose will not be accomplished." And I felt that this was so. I fought through this for about three nights; for about three nights I lay awake. But I believed God knew His own business, so I said, "Lord, if you want me to pray, you send them to me, and by the grace of God, I will do it." Since that time, thousands and thousands have been saved as a result of the healings, who might never have been saved otherwise—they might have died in their sins.

Dear friends, the people came and got convicted, saved, and healed. I have been in Chicago three times, and some of you know that the people came by the hundreds, rushing down the balconies, sides, and aisles.

The altar was full from one side to another. Everyone was trying to get there first. The whole place was crowded, and people tried to get in the back way.

The Power of God

In the first meeting in the big stone church, many hundreds came to be healed and saved, and they came so thick and fast that I could not stand it. I told the preachers that they had to help me. I called a brother over and said, "You take this chair and pray for the sick." He said, "Oh, I can't pray for the sick." I said, "Yes, you can. I will pray for you." He said, "Give me an easy one." I gave him the most seriously crippled person I could find, and I said, "Never mind, God can heal that one as easy as any."

They thought they were in for it. We had five chairs on that large platform, and two or three ministers to pray for the sick, but you would have been surprised to see how many were healed. It is Jesus who does it. When a few were healed, they had faith for the next one. It is wonderful how those people jumped and ran, shouting and praising God. Soon we had five rows of chairs, and I would go back and forth and encourage them. God did mighty works. The next place we go, we expect to see people coming by the hundreds.

Sometimes the power is very great when the saints are in one accord. People who are afflicted come to us from St. Louis, California, Alabama, and all over. Some come bringing their grave clothes along, but not one has died yet that we know of. Jesus is a mighty Savior. Sometimes the power has been so great that I have walked along large, long altars, telling the people, "I have no time to talk much. You know what to expect. The power of God is here. You give everything to God." In a few minutes, they would be leaping and running in all directions.

The power of God will go out like rivers of water. If you are looking to God in faith, you can get your baptism in the Spirit without waiting two or three weeks. It is not men or women, but God who does the work. Jesus Christ is the divine Healer and Baptizer. God gave Him power to give life to everyone who will come to God in His way.

In one meeting, they came by the hundreds, and we never could get around to each person individually. We only had two or three minutes, and there were fifty or one hundred people trying to come up. But the power of God was very great. By faith, we sprinkled the blood of Christ on them and looked to God. It was so late that I said, "The power of God will come, if you believe." I said, "By faith Moses took the blood of lambs and sprinkled the people, and I take the blood of the real Lamb, Calvary's Lamb, by faith, and sprinkle it over the people." I asked God to rebuke the diseases and take away people's sins. Right there, the power of God fell in every direction. God did the work. Oh, glory to God, who has given such wonderful powers to His church, through Jesus Christ, our Lord!

Chapter 5

The Power of the Word

The words of God have been sent down from heaven to us by Jesus Christ and the holy apostles, spoken by the Holy Spirit. They are from God, and they go forth a living power. Jesus said,

> *Believest thou not that I am in the Father, and the Father in me? the words that I speak unto you I speak not of myself: but the Father that dwelleth in me, he doeth the works. Believe me that I am in the Father, and the Father in me: or else believe me for the very works' sake.* (John 14:10–11)

Jesus also said that His works testified that the Father was in Him and with Him (John 10:38).

> *In the beginning was the Word, and the Word was with God, and the Word was God. The same was in the beginning with God. All things were made by him; and without him was not any thing made that*

was made....And the Word was made flesh, and dwelt
among us. (John 1:1–3, 14)

God spoke the worlds into existence. *"God said, 'Let there be light'; and there was light"* (Gen. 1:3 NKJV). As He spoke the Word, the earth, land, light, darkness, mighty seas, lakes, mountains, and valleys with all the fruits and flowers sprang into life, into existence and beauty. He spoke the Word, and every living creature stood before Him. From the mighty monsters of the sea, the lions of the forest, and the wild beasts of every kind, down to the little singing bird, they all stood looking in wonder and awe at the Mighty God who had, by the word of His mouth and the power of His voice, called them into this beautiful world. They said, by their very presence, "We know You are the great Jehovah, the God who inhabits eternity!"

The Words of God

That which was from the beginning, which we have heard, which we have seen with our eyes, which we have looked upon, and our hands have handled, of the Word of life; (for the life was manifested, and we have seen it, and bear witness, and show unto you that eternal life, which was with the Father, and was manifested unto us;) that which we have seen and heard declare we unto you, that ye also may have fellowship with us: and truly our fellowship is with the Father, and with his Son Jesus Christ.

(1 John 1:1–3)

When the high priest sent the officers to apprehend Jesus, the question was asked them, "Why did you not bring Him?" They said, *"Never man spake like this man"* (John 7:46). With His voice, the dead are raised and the lepers are cleansed. The blind see; they have their sight restored.

The raging storm on the Sea of Galilee was hushed at His word, and the roaring sea became as a sea of glass. The words of God spoken by the Holy Spirit have the same effect today. There is as much power in the name of Jesus today as in New Testament times. Through the Holy Spirit, His words come like coals of fire, burning through the minds and hearts of men. They are shot out like arrows dipped in the blood of Jesus; they are shot out like lightning, piercing the King's enemies in their heads and lodging in their hearts, so that they fall like dead men. They are like the little stones that David used to slay Goliath; we throw them at a venture, and God directs them so that they never return void (Isa. 55:11) but instead bring life or death, heaven or hell. They stand forever, for by the Word we will be justified or condemned.

When the disciples were arrested and put into prison, as recorded in Acts 5:19–20, *"the angel of the Lord by night opened the prison doors, and brought them forth, and said, Go, stand and speak in the temple to the people all the words of this life."* You see that God sent the angel to set them free and to tell them to go back, amid all the threats and danger, and preach *"all the words of this life."* His words are life; do not hold back any part of the message.

False Teachings

Jesus said, *"Whosoever therefore shall be ashamed of me and of my words...of him also shall the Son of man be ashamed, when he cometh in the glory of his Father"* (Mark 8:38). Oh, may God help all who pretend to preach the Word to see what is at stake! Will you please men or God? Will you deceive the people and come forward at the Judgment with your hands dripping with the blood of souls?

"Behold, the LORD's hand is not shortened, that it cannot save; neither his ear heavy, that it cannot hear" (Isa. 59:1).

> *For your hands are defiled with blood, and your fingers with iniquity; your lips have spoken lies, your tongue hath muttered perverseness....The way of peace they know not; and there is no judgment in their goings: they have made them crooked paths: whosoever goeth therein shall not know peace.*
>
> (vv. 3, 8)

Jesus is saying, "You have given them smooth sayings, trusting in good works and a moral life. You worship Me in vain, teaching the doctrines and traditions of men, which will perish with the using." (See Matthew 15:9.)

Jesus said what He will do when He comes in all His glory. Yes, He is coming soon. This is the time of the end; we see the signs everywhere. In this *"wicked and adulterous generation"* (Matt. 16:4), in these last days, the churches have gone after the wisdom and power of men, instead of the wisdom and power of God. *"Having a form of godliness, but denying the power thereof: from such turn away"* (2 Tim. 3:5). Read the third chapter of the second epistle of Timothy to gain an understanding of this.

God is calling as never before, in thunder tones, to those who pretend to preach His Word: "Blow the trumpet in Zion," and "sound an alarm in the Holy Mountain":

> *Blow ye the trumpet in Zion, and sound an alarm in my holy mountain: let all the inhabitants of the land tremble: for the day of the LORD cometh, for it is nigh at hand.* (Joel 2:1)

Let all the people tremble. What is the signal to make the people tremble? The Day of the Lord is at hand. It is even at your doors.

> *The great day of the LORD is near, it is near, and hasteth greatly, even the voice of the day of the LORD: the mighty man shall cry there bitterly. That day is a day of wrath, a day of trouble and distress, a day of wasteness and desolation, a day of darkness and gloominess, a day of clouds and thick darkness, a day of the trumpet and alarm against the fenced cities, and against the high towers. And I will bring distress upon men, that they shall walk like blind men, because they have sinned against the LORD: and their blood shall be poured out as dust, and their flesh as the dung. Neither their silver nor their gold shall be able to deliver them in the day of the LORD's wrath; but the whole land shall be devoured by the fire of his jealousy: for he shall make even a speedy riddance of all them that dwell in the land.* (Zeph. 1:14–18)

It Pays to Endure to the End

Hear the angel shout, "The hour of His judgment has come. Repent and worship God, who made heaven and earth and the sea and all that are therein." (See Revelation 14:7.)

The Holy Spirit

The time has come when men *"will not endure sound doctrine"* (2 Tim. 4:3), but are turning the people to *"cunningly devised fables"* (2 Pet. 1:16), turning away from the truth. They are *"men of corrupt minds, reprobate concerning the faith"* (2 Tim. 3:8), *"having a form of godliness, but denying the power thereof: from such turn away"* (v. 5). "Of him I will be ashamed when I come in all My glory." (See Mark 8:38.)

The last invitation is going forth, "Come to the Marriage of the Lamb and to the Supper of the Lamb." (See Revelation 19:9.) The Gospel of His coming kingdom is being preached as a witness to all nations (Matt. 24:14). This work will soon be done. What are you doing? Preach *"all the words of this life"* (Acts 5:20). Oh, what a calling! Oh, what a privilege! The angels who stand before the throne cannot do this work.

Jesus said, *"Tarry...until ye be endued with power from on high"* (Luke 24:49), and *"Ye shall receive power, after that the Holy Ghost is come upon you"* (Acts 1:8). Then you will

> cast out devils; [you] shall speak with new tongues; [you] shall take up serpents; and if [you] drink any deadly thing, it shall not hurt [you]; [you] shall lay hands on the sick, and they shall recover.
>
> (Mark 16:17–18)

People will have visions. Tell them that Jesus is coming soon. Show them the signs. The wise will know the times. (See Daniel 2:21–22; 12:10.) The wise will shine as the firmament (12:3). They will reign; they will be kings, with kingly authority, and will bless the people as priests for one thousand years. (See Revelation 20:6.)

The Power of the Word

The Bridal City

Do you not think that it will pay to be a true messenger, or herald, of His soon coming, when we will be like Him and will have glorious bodies like His? "Of such will I be well pleased when I come in all my Father's glory." (See Matthew 16:27.) Oh! Can you not understand? He is coming as the Prince of Glory to meet His bride in the air, to escort His bride back to the Great City, to be present at the Wedding, at the Marriage of the Lamb, when Jesus will present His bride to the Father. He will welcome His Son's wife. He is coming in all the glory of all His holy angels.

Oh, what a picture! Oh, what brightness! See, oh, see, the shining hosts! See Gabriel, who stands before God (Luke 1:19). They are getting ready. They are warming up the heavenly choir. They are coming. They are coming to meet us in the air! *"For the Lord himself shall descend from heaven with a shout, with the voice of the archangel, and with the trump of God: and the dead in Christ shall rise first"* (1 Thess. 4:16). They will come in the clouds of glory. We will all be caught up in the air, changed in a moment, have glorious bodies like our Lord and Savior, Jesus Christ, and be forever with the Lord (1 Thess. 4:17). Oh, this is wonderful, but it is true.

Don't Miss the Glory

Whosoever therefore shall be ashamed of me and of my words in this adulterous and sinful generation; of him also shall the Son of man be ashamed, when he cometh in the glory of his Father with the holy angels.
(Mark 8:38)

The Holy Spirit

Dear brothers and sisters in the ministry, can we miss this *"eternal weight of glory"* (2 Cor. 4:17)? When Jesus comes, will He be ashamed of us? The wicked will be completely ignored and banished from the Lord and from His glorious presence forever, because they were ashamed of Christ or of His words or of His supernatural and divine power or of the works of the Spirit, which are foolishness to the world and to the natural man. Will you miss all this for a high position or a high salary or a social position or to please the people? Oh, what will you do in that Day?

May God help us to preach *"all the words of this life"* (Acts 5:20) and *"earnestly contend for the faith...once delivered unto the saints"* (Jude 3).

As God sent Jesus into the world to deliver His messages, so Jesus sends us into the world as His ministers to preach the Gospel faithfully. Woe to us if we do not preach the whole truth or are ashamed or offended at any of His mighty works.

> *But though we, or an angel from heaven, preach any other gospel unto you than that which we have preached unto you, let him be accursed. As we said before, so say I now again, If any man preach any other gospel unto you than that ye have received, let him be accursed. For do I now persuade men, or God? or do I seek to please men? for if I yet pleased men, I should not be the servant of Christ. But I certify you, brethren, that the gospel which was preached of me is not after man. For I neither received it of man, neither was I taught it, but by the revelation of Jesus Christ.* (Gal. 1:8–12)

Notice that Paul said he had been taught by the revelation of Jesus Christ, by inspiration; no man had taught him. You see that the Bible is a sealed book to those who are lost. No one can preach the Gospel except by inspiration and revelation of the Holy Spirit through Jesus Christ, for He takes of the things of God and brings them to us; the Lord reveals them to us by His Spirit (John 16:13–15): *"But God hath revealed them unto us by his Spirit: for the Spirit searcheth all things, yea, the deep things of God"* (1 Cor. 2:10).

With man's wisdom, you can only learn historical knowledge and the dead letter that kills (2 Cor. 3:6) and condemns. However, the Spirit gives life (v. 6) and power. He takes into our hearts and minds thoughts from our loving Father, who says He will reveal His secrets to His sons. Jesus and the Father will come in and abide with us; they will manifest themselves to us. Oh, beloved, do not handle the Word of God deceitfully! Rather, as in the sight of God, preach the Word in the light and power of the Holy Spirit. Paul is our example. We should follow Paul as he followed Christ (1 Cor. 11:1):

> *I was with you in weakness, and in fear, and in much trembling. And my speech and my preaching was not with enticing words of man's wisdom, but in demonstration of the Spirit and of power.*   (1 Cor. 2:3–4)

> *For the gifts and calling of God are without repentance.*   (Rom. 11:29)

This song was composed by a minister sitting in the congregation, from a sermon preached on "The Great Day of His Wrath":

> In the awful day that's coming,
>   When Gabriel's trump shall sound

The Holy Spirit

And call the world to judgment,
   Oh! where shall we be found?
Shall we cry for the rocks and the mountains
   To hide us in that day,
From Him who comes in glory
   With all His bright array?

The Lord is coming shortly,
   According to His word,
Taking vengeance on the wicked
   And them that know not God.
Oh! who will then be able
   In that awful day to stand?
"Thou shalt be no longer steward!"
   Will be the stern command.

Shall we begin to tremble
   While looking on that sight
And take our march in anguish
   Down to eternal night?
Oh! what an awful picture!
   To some it will come true;
And, oh! my brother, sister,
   Shall it be I or you?

Chapter 6

The Prayer of Faith Will Save the Sick

Is any sick among you? let him call for the elders of the church; and let them pray over him, anointing him with oil in the name of the Lord: and the prayer of faith shall save the sick, and the Lord shall raise him up; and if he have committed sins, they shall be forgiven him. Confess your faults one to another, and pray one for another, that ye may be healed. The effectual fervent prayer of a righteous man availeth much. Elias was a man subject to like passions as we are, and he prayed earnestly that it might not rain: and it rained not on the earth by the space of three years and six months.
—James 5:14–17

The apostle James sent this letter out across the world to all churches, ministers, and members of the body of Christ. All these teachings and blessings are for every child of God who will accept them.

He wanted the church to know that the power to heal the sick and teach divine healing was not confined to the apostles, but that elders of each and every church had the gift of healing or the power to heal, and that by meeting the conditions given, every one of the followers of Christ would positively be healed.

He delivered this doctrine of divine healing of the body to be taught and practiced in every church, so that each member would know his privilege and duty to God. If he were sick, instead of sending only for a doctor, perhaps a non-Christian doctor, he should send at once for the elders and let God glorify Himself by manifesting the healing power in raising him up.

Some teachers refuse to walk in the God-given light, and they say that this text means spiritual healing. I am glad the Word of God is so plain that anyone who wants the light can have it. *"The prayer of faith shall save the sick, and the Lord shall raise him up; and if he have committed sins, they shall be forgiven him."* You see the line between the raising up of the sick one and the forgiving of sin. If the sick person has backslidden or sinned in any way that brought on the sickness, he should have faith in the promises of God in sending for the elders, as God has commanded.

The elders come and anoint with oil. This is a symbol of the Holy Spirit or healing power, which must come from Jesus, on and through the sick one—soul and body. They pray together the prayer of faith, and when they have met the conditions in this way, the Lord honors their faith. He comes with His mighty power and raises up the sick one to health and restores peace and joy in his soul. *"Pray one for another, that ye may be healed."*

The Prayer of Faith Will Save the Sick

You see that the power of the Lord is ever present with His children to heal. The command is given to every child of God. If the elders cannot come, then get a few of God's children together in the true Spirit of Christ and pray for one another so that you may be healed.

Some have gifts of casting out devils and healing by the laying on of hands. Oh, let us not forget these blood-bought benefits. "[He] *forgiveth all* [our] *iniquities;* [He] *healeth all* [our] *diseases*" (Ps. 103:3). He promises to heal soul and body; the verb is in the present tense: "*The effectual fervent prayer of a righteous man availeth much.*"

Unwavering Faith

The Lord shows us that we must have the righteousness of Christ, meet every other condition, and ask the Lord for what we want, in faith, without wavering. If we waver or doubt, we should not expect anything, for God will not hear us.

God will answer the prayer of faith, even if He has to bring all heaven down, in order to prompt us to greater faith to ask the Lord for greater things.

James referred us to the dark days of famine and condemnation in which Elijah lived, and he said, "[He] *was a man subject to like passions as we are.*" He was not an angel, but a man, with the same human nature and passions that we have. "*He prayed earnestly that it might not rain: and it rained not on the earth by the space of three years and six months.*" Elijah prayed again, and the rain came (James 5:18). He also prayed for God to send fire from heaven so that the people might know there was a true God, that he was God's servant, and that the Lord was leading him. (See 1 Kings 18.)

The Lord wants us to ask for great signs and wonders. The fire that came from heaven and brought the people down before God was a symbol of the Holy Spirit. The Lord wants to send signs and wonders into our midst, in answer to our prayers.

Elijah represents Christ—the church. When Elijah was taken up to heaven, a double portion of his spirit came upon Elisha, and Elisha did many more signs and wonders than Elijah did. Jesus said:

> *Verily, verily, I say unto you, He that believeth on me, the works that I do shall he do also; and greater works than these shall he do; because I go unto my Father. And whatsoever ye shall ask in my name, that will I do, that the Father may be glorified in the Son. If ye shall ask any thing in my name, I will do it.*
>
> (John 14:12–14)

> *If ye abide in me, and my words abide in you, ye shall ask what ye will, and it shall be done unto you.*
>
> (John 15:7)

You see, Christ's will and our wills come together with the same desire to glorify the Father. The Spirit of Christ prompts us to ask for great things so that the Lord will have a chance to let down His *"right hand of power"* (Matt. 26:64) and let the people see the visible signs of the *"LORD of hosts, which dwelleth in mount Zion"* (Isa. 8:18).

Every one of us ought to be anointed with the same power and gifts that God has given to the church, so that the world may believe that the Father has sent

The Prayer of Faith Will Save the Sick

Christ into the world and that the Father has loved us as He has loved Christ (John 17:23).

"In my name shall they cast out devils....They shall lay hands on the sick, and they shall recover" (Mark 16:17–18). These are the special gifts. I praise the Lord that He has given these gifts to me! In His name, through His name, thousands of unclean spirits have been cast out. Demons causing deafness, muteness, lameness, blindness, paralysis, and cancer have been driven out. Thousands of diseases have fled when I have laid my hands on the sick in His name; those who were sick have been made whole.

Healing in the Atonement

Divine healing is taught in the Atonement, as much as the salvation of the soul is. Consider these Scriptures:

> *He was wounded for our transgressions, he was bruised for our iniquities: the chastisement of our peace was upon him; and with his stripes we are healed.* (Isa. 53:5)

> *That it might be fulfilled which was spoken by Esaias the prophet, saying, Himself took our infirmities, and bare our sicknesses.* (Matt. 8:17)

Gifts and Workings of the Spirit

> *For to one is given by the Spirit the word of wisdom; to another the word of knowledge by the same Spirit; to another faith by the same Spirit; to another the gifts*

> *of healing by the same Spirit; to another the working of miracles; to another prophecy; to another discerning of spirits; to another divers kinds of tongues; to another the interpretation of tongues....For by one Spirit are we all baptized into one body....Ye are the body of Christ....God hath set some in the church* [body of Christ], *first apostles, secondarily prophets, thirdly teachers.* (1 Cor. 12:8–10, 13, 27–28)

Together we have the promise of apostles, prophets, teachers, and evangelists in the church of Christ. What a glorious church is the real body and bride of our Lord!

Signs were to follow those who believe in Christ (Mark 16:17): *"For the perfecting of the saints, for the work of the ministry, for the edifying of the body of Christ"* (Eph. 4:12). You see that God placed all the gifts and workings of the Spirit in the church, and they were to remain with the people of God *"till we all come in the unity of the faith"* (v. 13) *"by the same Spirit"* (1 Cor. 12:8). *"The manifestation of the Spirit is given to every man to profit withal....But all these worketh that one and the self-same Spirit"* (vv. 7, 11). There is one Lord and one Spirit (Eph. 4:4–5).

The Holy Spirit is the agent of Christ, sent by God to work through the church, the body of Christ. Each member is to possess one or more of these gifts as the church walks in the light and believes and accepts these blessings or gifts.

Ignorance Inexcusable

Paul said, *"Concerning spiritual gifts, brethren, I would not have you ignorant"* (1 Cor. 12:1). *"Till we all come in the unity of the faith, and of the knowledge of the Son of God, unto a perfect man, unto the measure of the stature of the fulness of Christ"* (Eph. 4:13).

Dearly beloved, when will we all come up to this measure? Not until the last one of the little flock is ready to be translated. We must be filled with the fullness of God, with wisdom and power. These signs and gifts must follow until the church goes out to meet the Lord, the Bridegroom. She will go out to meet Him with the same power that the apostles had after they were filled with the Holy Spirit on the Day of Pentecost. Oh, praise the Lord, all these signs are with us and are manifested in our meetings!

Chapter 7

Signs and Wonders to Lead People to Christ

All of us who have read the Acts of the Apostles know that the apostles' ministry was marvelously successful. Here are a few brief reports of some of their revivals from the book of Acts:

Then they that gladly received his word were baptized: and the same day there were added unto them about three thousand souls. (2:41)

And the Lord added to the church daily such as should be saved. (2:47)

Howbeit many of them which heard the word believed; and the number of the men was about five thousand. (4:4)

And believers were the more added to the Lord, multitudes both of men and women. (5:14)

The Holy Spirit

And the word of God increased; and the number of the disciples multiplied in Jerusalem greatly; and a great company of the priests were obedient to the faith. (6:7)

Then had the churches rest throughout all Judaea and Galilee and Samaria, and were edified; and walking in the fear of the Lord, and in the comfort of the Holy Ghost, were multiplied. (9:31)

While Peter yet spake these words, the Holy Ghost fell on all them which heard the word. (10:44)

And the hand of the Lord was with them: and a great number believed, and turned unto the Lord. (11:21)

But the word of God grew and multiplied. (12:24)

And the next sabbath day came almost the whole city together to hear the word of God. (13:44)

And so were the churches established in the faith, and increased in number daily. (16:5)

And some of them believed, and consorted with Paul and Silas; and of the devout Greeks a great multitude, and of the chief women not a few. (17:4)

Therefore many of them believed; also of honourable women which were Greeks, and of men, not a few. (17:12)

And fear fell on them all, and the name of the Lord Jesus was magnified. And many that believed came, and confessed, and showed their deeds. Many of them also which used curious arts brought their books

*together, and burned them before all men: and they
counted the price of them, and found it fifty thousand
pieces of silver. So mightily grew the word of God and
prevailed.*   (19:17–20)

Three Reasons for the Disciples' Success

There were three reasons or causes that gave the
disciples this phenomenal success.

First, they preached the Gospel of the kingdom,
which is, as I have already stated, a full Gospel for
spirit, soul, and body. They preached exactly as the
Lord told Jeremiah to preach:

*Thus saith the LORD: Stand in the court of the LORD's
house, and speak unto all the cities of Judah, which
come to worship in the LORD's house, all the words that
I command thee to speak unto them; diminish not a
word.*   (Jer. 26:2)

They also preached as the Lord told Jonah to preach:
*"And the word of the LORD came unto Jonah the second time,
saying, Arise, go unto Nineveh, that great city, and preach
unto it the preaching that I bid thee"* (Jonah 3:1–2).

The apostles did not diminish a word of the Gospel
of the kingdom. They preached precisely the Gospel
that Christ commanded them to preach. God will
always honor and bless such preaching.

In the second place, they preached this Gospel
under the power of the Holy Spirit, whom they had
received on the Day of Pentecost. This is such an
essential and all-important factor in preaching that
Jesus would not permit them to enter into their great

lifework until they had received the divine anointing. Had they not tarried in Jerusalem until this anointing came, the Acts of the Apostles would never have been written, for there would not have been any acts on their part that needed to be recorded, and the revivals mentioned above would never have been reported.

In the third place, God bore witness to their preaching with signs and wonders and with various miracles and gifts of the Holy Spirit (Heb. 2:4). This was as important a factor in their success as either of the others. I am convinced that without these miracles, the Gospel would have made but little progress in pushing its way through the heathen world.

Notice the apostles' prayer, which shows the estimation they placed upon miracles, especially the miracle of healing, as an auxiliary to their work:

> *And now, Lord, behold their threatenings: and grant unto thy servants, that with all boldness they may speak thy word, by stretching forth thine hand to heal; and that signs and wonders may be done by the name of thy holy child Jesus.* (Acts 4:29–30)

Notice now a significant fact. Read the following:

> *And by the hands of the apostles were many signs and wonders wrought among the people....Insomuch that they brought forth the sick into the streets, and laid them on beds and couches, that at the least the shadow of Peter passing by might overshadow some of them. There came also a multitude out of the cities round about unto Jerusalem, bringing sick folks, and them which were vexed with unclean spirits: and they were healed every one.* (Acts 5:12, 15–16)

Signs and Wonders to Lead People to Christ

The significant fact is that, in this passage, there is a parenthesis, which reads as follows:

> *(and they were all with one accord in Solomon's porch. And of the rest durst no man join himself to them: but the people magnified them. And believers were the more added to the Lord, multitudes both of men and women.)* (Acts 5:12–14)

Why did Luke insert that parenthesis? Did those miracles have anything to do with that multitude of believers, both men and women, being added to the Lord? They constituted a powerful factor in that revival. That was the result in nearly every instance: where miracles were performed, great revivals followed. Read these words:

> *And the word of God increased; and the number of the disciples multiplied in Jerusalem greatly; and a great company of the priests were obedient to the faith. And Stephen, full of faith and power, did great wonders and miracles among the people.* (Acts 6:7–8)

Is there any relationship between the miracles that Stephen worked and the multiplication of disciples in Jerusalem? There is a most intimate and vital relationship. Take another example:

> *Then Philip went down to the city of Samaria, and preached Christ unto them. And the people with one accord gave heed unto those things which Philip spake, hearing and seeing the miracles which he did. For unclean spirits, crying with loud voice, came out of many that were possessed with them:*

*and many taken with palsies, and that were lame,
were healed. And there was great joy in that city.*
(Acts 8:5–8)

Did the miracles of casting out unclean spirits and healing the lame have anything to do with the people giving heed with one accord to the things that Philip spoke and filling that city with joy? Very much. Take still another example:

*And it came to pass, as Peter passed throughout all
quarters, he came down also to the saints which dwelt
at Lydda. And there he found a certain man named
Aeneas, which had kept his bed eight years, and was
sick of the palsy. And Peter said unto him, Aeneas,
Jesus Christ maketh thee whole: arise, and make thy
bed. And he arose immediately. And all that dwelt at
Lydda and Saron saw him, and turned to the Lord.*
(Acts 9:32–35)

Raising Dorcas to life was another case that had the same effect (see verses 36–41): *"And it was known throughout all Joppa; and many believed in the Lord"* (v. 42).

If ministers could cast out devils today in the name of Jesus and lay hands on the sick and have them restored to health, they would not preach to empty benches or mourn over the dearth of revivals. On the contrary, every minister who could do that would have crowded houses and a perpetual revival. That is what God wants His ministers to do, and it is not His fault if they are not able to do it.

There is nothing the Devil hates with more infernal malevolence than divine healing. That is something that is visible, tangible, real, and valuable.

Signs and Wonders to Lead People to Christ

When a lame man is enabled to walk, or a poor epileptic is made well, that is something the unsaved world can see and appreciate. It convinces them of the goodness and loving-kindness of God.

A book is lying here in front of me. It is entitled, *Back to the Bible*. I've seen another book advertised, entitled, *Back to Pentecost*. Does it occur to these authors that to get back to the Bible and to Pentecost is to get back to miracle-working power?

Such a return would not only secure the baptism of the Spirit, but it would secure the gifts of the Spirit in the working of miracles. Is there anyone taking the track back in that direction?

Chapter 8

The Closing of the Gentile Age

The LORD shall rise up as in mount Perazim, he shall
be wroth as in the valley of Gibeon, that he may do
his work, his strange work; and bring to pass his act,
his strange act. Now therefore be ye not mockers, lest
your bands be made strong: for I have heard from the
Lord GOD of hosts a consumption, even determined
upon the whole earth.
—Isaiah 28:21–22

In all the history of the Bible, and in all God's deal-
ings with the world, He sent and offered mercy
and deliverance first and did everything to per-
suade people to trust and obey Him and escape the
coming judgments. But they still kept on sinning until
the pent-up wrath of God was poured out, and they
were all destroyed. Yet with a strong hand and a supernatural power, He was with His people in the *"spirit of*
justice" and *"strength"*—with *"those who turn*[ed] *back the*
battle at the gate" (Isa. 28:6 NKJV).

When mercy ceased to be a virtue, judgments came like a desolation, and destruction like a whirlwind. Hear what God said: "You will seek me very early, but your cries will come too late; I will not answer. I will laugh at your calamities and mock when your fear comes." (See Proverbs 1:26–30.)

In all the threatened dangers, and in the midst of awful judgments, the Lord caused His supernatural presence to be seen in signs through His children. While showing wrath, He worked His *"strange work"* through, and by, the Holy Spirit.

With all these past warnings and examples of mercy and awful calamities that came with or followed the loving voice of God—who so tenderly called people to Himself from their evil ways, called them to fly to His outstretched arms—with all these past warnings and examples, the poor, blinded, debauched world does not, and will not, take warning. Instead, after six thousand years, she keeps on sinning. She still seems to take the management from God, saying, "God does not know. He does not care. We will run the machinery ourselves."

People are running wild after wealth and status, worshipping the wisdom of men and their mighty inventive powers. Even in their professed worship, they have left the Fountainhead of living waters and have hewn out *"cisterns, broken cisterns, that can hold no water"* (Jer. 2:13). They have turned their backs to God and are facing the sun of human wisdom and power that has risen and blinded them so that they are satisfied with the gods of this world. (See 2 Corinthians 4:4.)

Hear one of the last warning notes from the eternal throne, from the loving Father: "In vain you worship

Me, going after the doctrines and traditions of men, which will perish with the using." (See Mark 7:7–9.)

The time for trifling is about over. God is calling modern-day Elijahs, who are clothed with the power of God, and King Ahabs to come face to face and test their gods. We must come to a halt and put our gods to a test. We will serve the one who answers by fire. That is God's test. (See 1 Kings 18:17–40.)

"It will come to pass in the last days," says the Lord, "that I will plead with all flesh, with the sword and fire, *and the slain of the Lord shall be many.*" (See Isaiah 66:16.)

The sword is the Word of God. The fire is the Holy Spirit. The slain of the Lord are those who fall under conviction or who fall like dead men under the power of God.

The Lightning of His Power

He will send out His arrows. His Word dipped in the blood of Jesus will be shot out with the lightning of His power, and the arrows will wound the King's enemies in the head. They will fall at His feet. Oh, praise His name. When God has His way, the ground of the meeting tent looks like a battlefield: men, women, and children lying everywhere, like dead men.

According to God's Word, the time of trouble, such as men have never seen or known, or ever will see again (Matt. 24:21), has already commenced and will end with the battle of the Great God.

We are in the last days of His preparation; Jesus is coming soon for His bride (1 Thess. 4:16–17), and she is getting ready. He is sending His angels, His servants, with the sound of a trumpet, calling the elect together, so that we may all be baptized with one faith, one Spirit, and one mind; so that we may be among the wise, who will *"shine as the brightness of the firmament"* (Dan. 12:3).

Isaiah 28, the chapter from which our text is taken, refers to the last church mentioned in the book of Revelation, the Laodicean church. This church is the *"vine of the earth"* (Rev. 14:18), the vine of man's planting. Jesus Christ shows us that in the awful destruction in which this *"vine"* will be utterly destroyed, the saints who are going through to victory will be clothed with power. (See Revelation 3:14–21.)

"The LORD shall rise up as in mount Perazim, he shall be wroth as in the valley of Gibeon, that he may do his work, his strange work," that He may work and bring to pass His strange acts in the last call of mercy. He will stir up the elements: *"Behold, the Lord hath a mighty and strong one, which as a tempest of hail and a destroying storm, as a flood of mighty waters overflowing, shall cast down to the earth with the hand"* (Isa. 28:2). He will bring distress upon men, because they have sinned against God, *"and their blood shall be poured out as dust, and their flesh as the dung. Neither their silver nor their gold shall be able to deliver them in the day of the LORD's wrath"* (Zeph. 1:17–18). He will rise in His wrath and work His *"strange work."*

God's Strange Acts in Old Testament Times

He will help His saints today, as he helped David at Mount Perazim and Gibeon. He will bring the powers of heaven, the destructive elements together, to accomplish His work through His saints.

The hosts of the enemies had gathered against David. He asked the Lord to help him. The Lord told him not to go near them but to take his forces back and to go under the mulberry trees and pay no attention to them. They were to rest and wait until he heard the sound of the *"going"* (2 Sam. 5:24) in the tops of the mulberry trees. Then he was to take his army and go forth to battle; he was to go after the enemy, for the Lord had gone before them, and He would smite the hosts of the Philistines.

The enemies heard the noise of the great hosts, the *"going"* in the treetops, the sound of war, of approaching armies. God confused them, and they were frightened, for they thought that David had engaged all the armies in the land against them.

It took great faith for David to obey the voice of God and to rest so peacefully under the trees when the hosts of enemies were ready to destroy them. But he knew that the battle was the Lord's (1 Sam. 17:47), and that, unless He fought for them, they were lost.

David was waiting for help from heaven; the armies of heaven were coming down to fight the battle. The Israelites had to wait until they heard the bugle blast, the rolling of chariots, the cannonading, and the noise of marching hosts. Oh, yes, our God of Battles gave them the victory, and their enemies fled before the Lord. (See 2 Samuel 5:17–25; 1 Chronicles 14:8–17.)

The Lord will also help his saints today as He helped Joshua. The enemy had gathered five kings with all their armies at Gibeon, and they were sure of victory.

They were trusting in the *"arm of flesh"* (2 Chron. 32:8), but the Mighty God of heaven was coming with His armies. *"And the LORD said unto Joshua, Fear them not: for I have delivered them into thine hand; there shall not a man of them stand before thee"* (Josh. 10:8).

As the armies fled from Israel, the Lord followed them and cast down great stones from heaven, so that more men died from the hailstones than by the sword (v. 11).

The Lord God will work His *"strange work"* for us, as in Gibeon. The battle was on; the enemy was strong, and defeat was sure, unless the God of Battles came to the rescue. The only hope was for God to work a miracle, to do a *"strange act."*

Then the Lord told Joshua to command the sun to stand still, and the sun stood still in the midst of the heavens; it did not go down for a whole day. The Lord told Joshua to command the moon to stand still and not to go down until they had gained a victory. There had never been a day like it, in which the Lord listened to the voice of a man. The Lord fought for them. (See Joshua 10:1–15.)

The Lord says He will *"rise up"* in wrath and work His *"strange work,"* His strange acts, as He did in Gibeon; the whole land will be destroyed. He will make a speedy riddance of the whole land. Two-thirds of the tribes of the earth will perish (Zech. 13:8) by storms, earthquakes, hail, cyclones, floods, pestilence, and famine in this time of trouble. (See Matthew 24:7; Revelation 16:18, 21.)

And there fell upon men a great hail out of heaven, every stone about the weight of a talent [one hundred pounds or more]: *and men blasphemed God because of the plague of the hail; for the plague thereof was exceeding great.* (Rev. 16:21)

God's Strange Acts in the Early Church

God is pouring out His Spirit in these last days (Acts 2:17) of the *"latter rain"* (Joel 2:23), and His people are seeking and receiving the baptism of the Holy Spirit with all the Pentecostal gifts and blessings. God has risen up and is working His *"strange work,"* His strange acts, the acts of the apostles, through His baptized saints.

When the paralytic was healed by Jesus and took up his bed and walked, all the people shouted with a loud voice, giving glory to God. The fear of God fell on all. They walked softly, saying, "We have seen strange things today." (See Mark 2:1–12.) Oh, praise God. Praise His holy name forever and ever.

When the Holy Spirit came on the Day of Pentecost like a rushing wind, this was His *"strange act,"* similar to bringing His hosts of armies through the treetops. When the tongues of fire rested on the heads of the hundred and twenty disciples, and they were all filled with the Holy Spirit and began to speak in other tongues as the Spirit gave utterance (Acts 2:4), this was God's *"strange act,"* His *"strange work."* (See Acts 2:1–4.)

While Peter was preaching at the home of Cornelius, the Holy Spirit was poured out on everyone, and they spoke with new tongues and magnified God. This was His *"strange work,"* His *"strange act."* (See Acts 10.)

The Holy Spirit

This is the day; this is the time spoken of. He has risen up in majesty, like a mighty *"man of war"* (Isa. 42:13) and of power.

Hear the Spirit of the Conqueror, "Come up, my people, come up to the help of the Lord, against the mighty." The Devil is mighty in these last days, but *"the battle is the Lord's"* (1 Sam. 17:47).

The hosts of evil have not only gathered against us, but against the Lord of Hosts. The *"captain of the LORD's host"* (Josh. 5:15) has come down to fight our battles. He is in our midst. He goes before us with a *"two-edged sword"* (Rev. 1:16 NKJV); He has bowed the heavens and come down (Ps. 144:5). He is making the people tremble. He is moving the mountains of difficulty and of sin, of tumors and of cancers. He is tearing down the Devil's works and breaking the hearts of stone. (See Ezekiel 11:19.) Yes, the Lord is bringing the powers of heaven and the destroying elements together. They are rising up in His wrath.

When His judgments are in the earth, some will repent. Yes, we see the great calamity, the sinking of the mighty *Titanic*, causing travail and gloom and sorrow and awakening people all over the world. We see great loss of life in floods, fires, and earthquakes. We see the terrifying storms and cyclones. Men and women turn pale from fear and from watching and wondering what will happen next. Yes, the Lord is working through the elements and through the *"strange work"* of the Holy Spirit through His children: the great work of giving the last warning, the last call, for people to escape these things that are coming upon the earth and to stand before the Lord at His coming (Luke 21:36).

The Lord is sending His angels, His saints, with the sound of a great trumpet. The Gospel is the trumpet, and it is blown in Zion. *"Blow ye the trumpet in Zion, and sound an alarm in my holy mountain"* (Joel 2:1). Let all the people tremble. The great Day of the Lord is near; it is near, even at your doors. (See Matthew 24:33.) It is the last call to be saved before the *"great and notable day of the Lord come*[s]*"* (Acts 2:20).

> *Therefore be ye not mockers, lest your bands be made strong: for I have heard from the Lord G**od** of hosts a consumption, even determined upon the whole earth.*
> (Isa. 28:22)

We can all see the *"strange work"* in the workings of the Holy Spirit through, and with, the baptized saints. As it was in the early church, this "sect" is spoken against everywhere (Acts 28:22). The workings of the Holy Spirit are foolishness to men. People cry out and say, "They are drunk." However, they do not mean that they are drunk with wine or strong drink. They say, "They are hypnotized and mesmerized." Many are mockers. They see the strange and supernatural with the natural eye, and they hear with their ears the wonderful works of God. They confess that there was and is great power demonstrated. They cannot deny the great miracles. It makes them fear and tremble. But many turn away, drive away their conviction, and become mockers.

They commit the unpardonable sin, and their chains are made strong; they are lost forever. The Lord says He will consume them in His wrath. They will not mock then, when the tornado is raging, when the earth is rocking and reeling under the earthquake. But now they greatly mock, and they say of the strange and supernatural, "It is true that a work has been done, but it is the work of the Devil."

The Holy Spirit

In his vision, Daniel heard one saint ask another, "When will all these wonders cease?" The answer was, "When the shattering of the power of the holy people has been accomplished, all these wonders will cease." (See Daniel 12:5–7.) The Gospel of His coming kingdom must first be preached, as a witness to all nations (Matt. 24:14). God will have many witnesses out of every nation, tongue, and people on the earth.

Signs, Wonders, and Works

These signs, wonders, works, and demonstrations, and the power of the Holy Spirit, must be dispersed through baptized saints. This is our work today: calling the elect together, so that they may see, feel, and receive the baptism of the Spirit and be sealed with the knowledge of God; so that they may be among the wise who will know when Jesus is coming. (See Daniel 2:21–22; 12:10.) Then they will shine like the sun in our Father's kingdom (Matt. 13:43).

The Lord of Hosts is with us today *"for a crown of glory, and for a diadem of beauty, unto the residue of his people"* (Isa. 28:5) and with great power *"to those who turn back the battle at the gate"* (v. 6 NKJV).

He is giving His wisdom to the weak. To those who do not naturally have the wisdom of this world, He is teaching knowledge and bringing understanding. To those who are weaned from the milk—little children and those who are not learned—He is revealing and manifesting Himself. Yes, He reveals the *"deep things of God"* (1 Cor. 2:10), causing us to speak in new tongues as the Spirit gives utterance (Acts 2:4), showing the *"wonderful works of God"* (v. 11).

The Closing of the Gentile Age

He is speaking in other languages—fluently, plainly, distinctly, and with power—what no one can learn at school, except after a long time. "With stammering lips and other tongues I will speak unto this people, yet for all that, you will not believe." (See Isaiah 28:11–12.) Oh, readers, do not be mockers, lest your chains be made strong, lest you be consumed. Hear Him say so. Hear, friend.

The apostle Paul referred to the above warning hundreds of years after it was solemnly spoken by the prophet. (See 1 Corinthians 14:21–22.) The outpouring of the Spirit in the gift of tongues is one of the last signs God is giving to the lost world that He is moving in our midst and that Jesus is coming. Yes, it is a special sign that Jesus is coming soon. Yet with all this, you will not believe. Be careful how you hear and how you act. It is the last call. God is working His *"strange work"* and His *"strange act."* The Holy Spirit is seen in many ways. He is seen in bright lights, in balls of fire, in hundreds of stars, and in companies of angels, over and in the tent in our meetings.

The Lord of Hosts says He will work as He did when the sun and moon stood still at the command of Joshua. We will not be surprised at anything our God does. His people are a people of power. *"All thy works shall praise thee, O Lord; and thy saints shall bless thee. They shall speak of the glory of thy kingdom, and talk of thy power"* (Ps. 145:10–11).

Chapter 9

"Will You Also Go Away?"

Jesus said, *"As the living Father hath sent me, and I live by the Father: so he that eateth me, even he shall live by me"* (John 6:57). If a person keeps on eating and believing, he will never die spiritually: *"This is that bread which came down from heaven: not as your fathers did eat manna, and are dead: he that eateth of this bread shall live for ever"* (v. 58).

Many of His followers said, *"This is an hard saying; who can hear it?"* (v. 60). Jesus knew their murmuring, and He gave them a little insight into the great Resurrection: *"What and if ye shall see the Son of man ascend up where he was before?"* (v. 62). He added, *"Therefore said I unto you, that no man can come unto me, except it were given unto him of my Father"* (v. 65). That is a wonderful truth. No man ever made his way to Jesus without God. No man ever made his way to Jesus unless the Father sent His Spirit and drew him.

"From that time many of his disciples went back, and walked no more with him. Then said Jesus unto the twelve, Will ye also go away?" (vv. 66–67). I don't think Jesus was ever more sad than at that moment. He saw the

multitude turn away; they would not walk in the light. Peter answered Him, *"Lord, to whom shall we go? thou hast the words of eternal life. And we believe and are sure that thou art that Christ, the Son of the living God"* (vv. 68–69).

Many do not believe that today. Many do not know it, but that is the key to the whole Word of God: *"And we believe and are sure that thou art that Christ, the Son of the living God."*

"As the living Father hath sent me, and I live by the Father" (v. 57)—we must live in the same way, by the power of Almighty God. Glory to God.

We can see by what we have read that the Lord had many thousands of followers by this time. His fame had gone out all over the land. He had five thousand converts when He supplied them with bread in the wilderness. Another time, there were seven thousand who saw the mighty power of Almighty God through Jesus Christ when they ate and were filled, and many basketfuls were taken up from what remained of the few loaves and fishes with which they had started. Thousands came to Him for salvation and healing; when they were healed, they always received salvation. He gave them the double cure.

Christ said, "Which is easier: to take away sins or heal the body?" (See Mark 2:9.) One is as easy as the other. After He healed the invalid at the pool of Bethesda, He said, *"Behold, thou art made whole: sin no more, lest a worse thing come unto thee"* (John 5:14). The people Christ healed got the double cure: they were saved and healed. They were pretty well acquainted with Christ and His love and mercy and mighty power. They had heard of His fame, and every day His power was greater and more wonderfully demonstrated.

"Will You Also Go Away?"

One day, when Jesus and His disciples were in a boat, a great storm arose. The waves were going over the ship; it was going down, and everyone was about to be drowned. Yet when the disciples had faith to come and call Him, He stepped out and said, *"Peace, be still"* (Mark 4:39). The mighty wind ceased, and the rolling waves suddenly became as a sea of glass through the mighty power of Christ. The mighty power of God fell upon the disciples, and they came forward and said, "Behold, what manner of man is He anyway? Is there no limit to His mighty power? This Man, this Messiah, says He is the Son of God. We are following Him from day to day, and every day we see more of His mighty power. There is no limit to it; even the winds and the waves obey Him." (See verse 41.) Everyone on the ship fell at His feet and acknowledged Him as the Son of God.

So His fame went everywhere, not so much because of what He said, but because of the mighty manifestations.

Jesus said, "If you don't believe what I say, believe Me for the works' sake. (See John 14:11.) They testify that I came from God and am the Son of the living God. (See John 5:36; 10:25, 38.) Even though I spoke as no man has ever spoken (see John 7:46), you seem to have a cloak around you; however, before the mighty signs and wonders, you stand before God naked."

The people had seen the mighty miracles; they had heard Him speak; they had seen His majesty and power in so many ways. But now He began to tell them about being filled with God, giving themselves up to the fullness of God, being baptized with the Holy Spirit, being kept by the authority of God.

The Holy Spirit

Jesus said, *"I live by the* [living] *Father"* (John 6:57). He was sustained and kept continually by the power and presence of the living God, for the Father never left Him for a moment. He said, "The works that I do, I do not do, but my Father does the works. The words I say, I do not say, but my Father gives me the words. (See John 14:10.) Whatever the Father tells me to do, I do." He gave the Father credit for everything.

He was sustained by the mighty power of the living God, and we also must come to the point where we can be sustained and kept in the same way, by the power of God through Jesus Christ. This is a hard saying; who therefore can be saved? (See Matthew 19:25.) We are not to live by natural bread alone (Matt. 4:4); to get to heaven, the spiritual man must be sustained and fed by the Bread of Heaven, by the Holy Spirit. We need to drink from the Fountain that never runs dry.

The sixth chapter of John shows us that many of Jesus' followers did not understand this and did not want to. In the same way, many people today don't want to walk in the light, and they turn away and are lost forever. The question is, *"Who then can be saved?"* (Matt. 19:25).

The people in Jesus' day began to murmur and grumble as they do today. God knows when people grumble. Many thousands of those people who were saved and had had all those blessings, turned away and never followed the Son of God anymore. Jesus looked at the few who were left, and His heart must have been broken for those who were so blind. He asked His disciples, "Will you also go away?"

He is saying the same thing to us. So many Christians have backslidden and are going off into delusions. It is the sifting time as never before. God is looking at us, especially those who are baptized in the Spirit. He asks, "Will you also forsake Me? Will you also turn back, or will you go forward all the way?" Peter's answer was, "'To whom shall we go?' (John 6:68). We cannot find a better way. This has been a glorious way, and we are willing to go all the way. 'Thou hast the words of eternal life' (v. 68). We don't guess—'we believe and are sure that thou art that Christ, the Son of the living God' (v. 69)."

Earlier, Jesus had said to those who were offended by His words, "What if you should see Me ascend to heaven?" (See verse 62.) He wanted to show them the mighty power of the Holy Spirit. He wanted to show the resurrection life and that the saints would go up by the same power. "I am the Living Bread that comes down from heaven; he who eats of Me will live by Me, and if he continues to eat, he will never die spiritually." (See verse 51.)

They Laughed at the Signs

Jesus said to the few who remained, "Will ye also go away?" (v. 67). And they answered, "We know truly that You are the Christ, the Son of the living God, whom you have been telling us about." (See verse 69.)

Oh, glory to God! Dear friends, God's people were always the fewest of all the people on earth. God said to the children of Israel, "I did not choose you because you were the wisest or the wealthiest people; you were the fewest of all the people on the earth. Yet I have called you, chosen you, put my love upon you." (See Deuteronomy 7:6–8.) We find that the previous followers of the Lord God always diminished instead of increased. We find that, way back at the beginning, at the time of the Flood, when the ark finally sailed away, only eight souls had faith enough to sail away with it, and all the rest went down to an awful doom. They saw the mighty signs and wonders, but they would not believe God. They laughed at the sign. They thought that Noah was a fool and that the ark was the craziest building they had ever seen. They turned away after having had the light.

Even before the great inferno on the plain of the Jordan, when the judgments and fire of God came down and destroyed the proud cities of Sodom and Gomorrah, God sent an angel from heaven to warn the people, but only three souls escaped to the mountains. The people had their chance; they had their opportunity. But they turned back; they took the wrong way. God gave mercy first, until finally His mercy ceased. They lost their opportunity; judgments came. Judgments have always followed and always will follow the backslider who refuses to obey God. It is judgment unto death. Where Christ is, the disobedient can never go. We find that all through the Word of God, there were just a few who obeyed God. At the destruction of Jerusalem, the people had the call, they all had a chance, but not many escaped.

Only Twelve Left

Now I want to come back to my main point. I said earlier that after the multitudes abandoned Christ, and there were only twelve disciples left, Jesus asked these few, *"Will ye also go away?"* (John 6:67). Peter answered, *"Lord, to whom shall we go? thou hast the words of eternal*

"Will You Also Go Away?"

life" (v. 68). The rest never followed Him anymore; we never hear of them. These people had been saved, but they did not follow the Son of God anymore.

After Jesus rose from the dead, He appeared to His disciples. He asked for fish and ate it in their presence. He called Thomas to come and put his finger into His side, and He proved to them that He had the same body that had been laid in the grave. Many different times, He appeared to them to take away every doubt and prove that He was the risen Christ, the Son of the living God, and would soon ascend back to God where He came from. Different times, He met with them. At one time after He rose from the dead, He was seen by five hundred disciples.

Many believe that this instance was the time He ascended to heaven. He went out on the mountain, talked to His disciples for the last time, and gave the Great Commission. (See Matthew 28:16–20.) The disciples watched Him ascending into heaven until the angels appeared and said, *"Why stand ye gazing up into heaven? this same Jesus, which is taken up from you into heaven, shall so come in like manner as ye have seen him go into heaven"* (Acts 1:11). And they remembered that He had charged them, "Don't preach sermons or teach the people or do anything, but wait at Jerusalem until you have been endued with power from on high." (See Luke 24:49.) They had a great deal to preach about concerning Christ's sufferings, death, and resurrection, but He told them, "You will not have entered into this wonderful life until you have been endued with power from on high."

Glory to God! I want you to see that Christ wanted to select men and women to set up His spiritual kingdom. He wanted to qualify them to establish the Holy

Spirit religion in the world. But after all they had seen and heard, and after these five hundred had seen Jesus and were thoroughly convinced that He was the Son of God, there were only one hundred and twenty out of the five hundred, to say nothing about any of the rest, who really believed and were willing to face the music—to face death or anything else—until God qualified and sent them out.

It seems as if His work may have diminished after He was taken to heaven. May God help you to see whose fault it was that some did not come to the Upper Room and wait to be initiated into the Holy Spirit baptism and the secrets of heaven. Perhaps only the one hundred and twenty who were present in the Upper Room believed that God would fulfill the promise made hundreds of years earlier to the prophets, a promise that Jesus had confirmed. When the Day of Pentecost came, there was only a small company of disciples there with God to be qualified to establish the Holy Spirit church. They were saved and full of joy; they believed they would receive the Holy Spirit, and they went back to Jerusalem and waited, continually blessing and praising God. They were filled with joy. If you are seeking the baptism, get saved first, get filled with joy, get off the judgment seat, and be of one accord, of one mind, praising the Lord, just as the early believers were. (See Acts 1:14; 2:1.)

A Blaze of Pentecostal Power

Christ's church was set up in a blaze of Pentecostal power. Common, unlearned men and women went to the Upper Room trusting God, and the power of heaven came down. (See Acts 2:1–4.) They knew God was coming, and they were not being critical about how He would come, but were willing to leave all that in God's hands. Suddenly, while they were praising and blessing God, they heard a sound from heaven like a *"rushing mighty wind"* (Acts 2:2). The whole building was shaken, and the tidal wave filled the place. The power of God struck them, and the Holy Spirit came to rest on each of them like tongues of fire.

God was initiating them into the *"deep things of God"* (1 Cor. 2:10) and making them pillars in the church of the living God (Rev. 3:12). This was where the church was established, where the church was organized, the *"church of the firstborn"* (Heb. 12:23). Glory to God! These few disciples were all that the Lord had to depend on to establish the church and spread the glad news of what had happened. "You will receive power after the Holy Spirit has come upon you, and then you will know how to testify of Me. (See Acts 1:8.) Tell them in a way that people will believe. I will be with you always (Matt. 28:20), and when you preach the Word, you will see the signs of the living Christ right in your midst."

Glory to God! Filled with the Holy Spirit, they began to preach the wonderful things, and the Lord Jesus Christ was with them. He was there invisibly. He was the Coworker with them, and He is working with His saints today. The Lord Jesus Christ confirms the Word with signs and wonders following. (See Mark 16:20.)

However, when the news went out, and the crowds came to see what was taking place on the Day of Pentecost, they said that these people were all drunk. They began to lie about the Holy Spirit, and they have been lying ever since. Peter quoted the ancient prophets and said, "You believe the prophets; then hear what they say. This is exactly what they said was coming, what God said would take place in the last days. What you are seeing with the natural eye and what you are hearing (and we know they felt it)—this is the power of God. It is the Holy Spirit sent down from heaven." (See Acts 2:5–18.)

But the great company that had followed Jesus previously and seen the mighty miracles refused to walk in the light. When we are born of the Spirit, we have some of the light of heaven in our souls. Jesus is giving us more light, and He is giving us degrees of glory. As long as we walk in that light, we have fellowship with one another, and the blood of Jesus Christ, His Son, cleanses us from sin (1 John 1:7).

You are either going forward or backward. As long as you walk in the light, you have fellowship with and love for your brothers and sisters in Christ, and you have a present salvation. However, when you refuse to walk in the light, you go backward, and you lose that sweet fellowship with God and with the saints.

God is testing us, just like He did the Jews, down to the end of the age. Christ will not return until there is a falling away from the faith (2 Thess. 2:3). God knows there is a falling away today. The church of Jesus Christ was inaugurated in a blaze of glory and celestial fireworks, but she must be taken up in a greater blaze of glory. *"Fear not, little flock; for it is your Father's good pleasure to give you the kingdom"* (Luke 12:32). The Holy Spirit will continue to take us down into the *"deep things of God"* (1 Cor. 2:10), and we will be filled with all the fullness of God, with our garments white (Rev. 3:5) and our lamps brightly burning. (See Matthew 25:1–13.)

"Will You Also Go Away?"

The church will soon leave this world in a cloud of glory. God is calling out a people for a prepared place (John 14:2–3), and He is preparing a people to finish up His work in the church of the living God. She must be a glorious church, pure and white and clothed with the power of Almighty God—a prepared people, a special nation, a called-out nation from all the nations of the earth, a separate nation, a holy priesthood (1 Pet. 2:9), children of the living God, God's sons and daughters.

So now, the Lord is calling us to eat the *"strong meat"* (Heb. 5:14). He is calling the saints of God to get deeper in Him. We must be filled with the Holy Spirit; we must eat of the Living Bread. By continuing to eat, we will never die spiritually. The time has come in which we must have strong meat. We must receive it or be left behind in the Great Tribulation that is coming. One calamity after another is sweeping over the earth. Unless we get deep in God, the waves and tribulations will sweep us away. Blessed is that servant whom Jesus will find giving the saints of God their *"meat in due season"* (Matt. 24:45) when He comes to catch His bride away. This Gospel of His kingdom must be preached to all nations, and then the end will come (v. 14). This Gospel must be backed up by mighty signs and wonders, by people filled with the Holy Spirit, baptized in the fire.

Refusing to Walk in the Light

People don't want to walk in the light; they don't like the way. They say, "We will be despised, and they will call us all kinds of names." If they can call us any worse than they did the Son of God, I'd like to know about it. But if we suffer with Him, we will reign with Him (2 Tim. 2:12). He has promised us everything in this life, *"with persecutions"* (Mark 10:30). We all want the good things but not the persecution. Yet those who desire to live in a godly way will suffer persecution (2 Tim. 3:12). Bless God, He is around us like a wall of fire. He who is in us and around us is greater than he who is against us (1 John 4:4).

Will you belong to the royal line? Will you accept the invitation and eat of the *"strong meat"* (Heb. 5:14)? Will you be baptized in the Holy Spirit? May God help us to say yes. Will you go on the mountaintop and help make up the little flock that will fill the earth with a blaze of glory? The wise, those who know the *"deep things of God"* (1 Cor. 2:10), will shine as the sun (Matt. 13:43) when Jesus comes. Those who are wise will even outshine the sun. Don't you see how you can glorify God? He is coming *"in the glory of his Father"* (Matt. 16:27), in the glory of all the angels. He is coming for His bride. The saints who are alive in that day will be taken up alive. *"We shall not all sleep, but we shall all be changed"* (1 Cor. 15:51). Bless God! He makes our feet like hinds' feet (2 Sam. 22:34). He makes us jump and dance with joy. It is the resurrection power.

You say, "Oh, I don't want to be a fool." But you are one already. I would rather be a fool for God than for the Devil. To everyone who is not saved, He says, *"Thou fool"* (Luke 12:20). I would rather be one of God's wise little ones, even if all the people in the world called me a fool. For the wisdom of this world is foolishness in the sight of God (1 Cor. 3:19). The wisdom of this world will perish. Men are trusting in their money and education and the like instead of trusting in the arm of Almighty God. All these things will perish. But look at the Great

White Throne (Rev. 20:11); see the River of Life (Rev. 22:1); see the wonderful things God is preparing. The things we see here will perish, but the things we see in the Spirit up in heaven will last forever.

God will gather us up and take us where the people never get old! There will be no death! No children will be crying for bread! There will be no prairie fires! No wars! Bless God, we are going! Don't you want to join the procession? Don't you want to sell everything and go? Leave the city of destruction and run from the storm; don't linger in the plain. Prepare to meet God. Prepare for the coming of the Lord, because He is coming.

Let us not be foolish, like the great company of those disciples who had the light. Some had been healed; many had been saved. They had come to know that God is good. But people are saying today, as they said then, "Have any of the priests believed? No, not many? Well, I guess I won't then, either." There will be some priests who will go to hell; ministers will, too, if they don't get right with God. Priests and ministers all have to go the same way, through the narrow gate; they have to wash in the fountain and be made white in order to receive eternal life. If you expect to go up, you must wait at your Jerusalem and be filled. In heaven, we won't be mortal or in the grave; the Holy Spirit will quicken our mortal bodies. Like David, we will say, *"For by thee I have run through a troop; and by my God have I leaped over a wall"* (Ps. 18:29).

God gives you power to dance, power to get out of the mud and run up the mountains. Bless God! Let us get out of the mud. Let us get cleaned up and dressed up for heaven. Join this race. God is filling the people. There are great degrees of glory, but everyone can advance another degree, and another, and another—and they won't have to pay any money, either—until they come into the perfect image of Jesus Christ. (See 2 Corinthians 3:18.) But you say, "I don't want to give up this, and I don't want to give up that." If you had any of the love of God in your heart, you would not want to do these things, because you would be a new creature. Old things would pass away, and everything would be new (2 Cor. 5:17). But the trouble is that you don't want to walk in the light.

Stubborn or Fearful

Many people see the light, but they are too stubborn to walk in it. They don't want to follow that path and be laughed at and all that. Dear friends, what do you care? How many of you draw back through fear—fear of being laughed at, fear that you will lose your position or be "thrown out of the synagogue"? (See John 9:22.) Bless God, they cannot throw you out of heaven.

God is pouring out His Spirit; many have had the real Pentecostal power, but they are not willing to acknowledge it. They are not willing to go forward, and they begin to draw back, sinning against the light. Refusing to walk in the light, they get leanness of soul. The first thing you know, if you fail to walk in the light, you cease to have fellowship with Jesus, the blood ceases to cleanse, and you begin to invent excuses to ease your own guilty conscience. (See 1 John 1:7–8.) You were not willing to acknowledge that you did not know it all. "Behold, I show you a new thing." (See Isaiah 43:19.) You did not know it yesterday. "Behold, I will show you new things from this day. Things you never knew

"Will You Also Go Away?"

before." So many of us do not want to acknowledge that we don't know it all. We don't know anything as we ought to, and there is so much more for us. Let us leave the shoreline and get where the Spirit lets us down into the deep things of God.

People are not willing to walk in the light. Thousands of people who have come up against the Pentecostal movement have declared that it is of the Devil or something similar, and when we refuse to walk in the light, it is death to our souls, especially if we "lay hands on the ark." It is spiritual death to that man's soul if he does not make it right. (See 2 Samuel 6:2–7.)

So there is great confusion. At the same time, there are a great many who have just been saved and who are being filled with God and baptized in the Holy Spirit. God is revealing wonderful things to them, and they are going on and on in the Lord, thanking God for what they have and advancing in glory. Some are in a place of affliction, where everything is against them—all the Devil's old rubbish. It is the sifting time. They are going upstream, but they will land on the mountaintop when Jesus comes to catch His bride away. We find that after Jesus takes the saints away, He will come back with them, and they will return on white horses. Imagine this little flock coming back on white horses!

Jesus is coming back! We are told that He is coming on a great white horse with a great army from heaven behind Him, all on white horses (Rev. 19:11–14). The bride of Christ will be shouting glory to Him who bought us with His own blood. This little flock will be taken up very soon. Jesus will take them away from earth and bring them home to heaven. He will make them kings and priests to God, and they will reign for one thousand years (Rev. 20:6).

The Holy Spirit

At Pentecost, when the few out of many thousands were willing to be called fanatics, then God, true to His promise, owned and accepted them with a cloudburst of glory and filled their bodies with the Holy Spirit. God spoke through them in other languages. They were ignorant, unlearned people, but God took possession of them and got hold of their tongues and spoke through them, as He had said He would: *"With stammering lips and another tongue will* [I] *speak to this people"* (Isa. 28:11); yet for all that, some don't want to hear (v. 12). The believers at Pentecost could afford to be laughed at and eventually brought to death, in order to have such a visitation from heaven and to have God smile on them.

A Royal Line

Jesus must become to us the fairest *"among ten thousand"* (Song 5:10) and the *"altogether lovely"* One (v. 16), and we must be willing to leave everything and everyone on earth to follow Him. The great holy Bridegroom is getting ready to come and take away His bride. *"Fear not, little flock; for it is your Father's good pleasure to give you the kingdom"* (Luke 12:32).

Are we going to backslide instead of walking in the light? Are we going to eat the *"strong meat"* (Heb. 5:14), or are we going to say the way is too hard and go off and grumble and growl and be lost forever? We are a royal line, the King's sons and daughters, a company of nobles, children of the living God who will go up to meet Christ—a great company. Every last one of us will be a king and a priest. Bless God, we are going to ride on the white horses and come back to the great Battle of Armageddon. But we must have the white robes on down here and follow the Lord wherever He goes.

If you are persecuted for Christ's sake, *"great is your reward in heaven"* (Matt. 5:12). However, if you are persecuted because you are walking in a crooked way, you ought to be persecuted enough to humble yourself and get right with God. If you are wrong, it will take persecution to get you right, but if you are a child of God and these persecutions come, then you can look up and rejoice because *"great is your reward in heaven."*

Jesus is coming soon. He is giving you an invitation to the Wedding. Will you accept it? Will you be one of the little flock? The angels are holding back the four winds (see Revelation 7:1) and they are crying, "Shall we let loose?" No, not until we have sealed the servants of God in the forehead with the seal of the living God. (See Ezekiel 9:4; Revelation 7:3.) Perhaps you are a servant of God; you need to be sealed, baptized, filled with new life. One of these days, we will burst these chains and go up to meet the Lord in the air. You who love Jesus will be tested. God is asking us the question: "Will you go away also?"

Is the way too hard? Is the price too great? Make up your mind that you will stand on the rock and that even if the whole world leaves, you won't, because Christ will be sufficient. We are going to be tested as never before. It is going to be harder every day, even among the people of God, because so many false teachers are coming in. It is a day of delusions; all kinds of delusions are coming. Keep under the blood, keep white, keep holy, keep pure, and God will give us wisdom. Glory to God!

Chapter 10

The Great Revival in Jerusalem

And great fear came upon all the church, and upon
as many as heard these things. And by the hands of
the apostles were many signs and wonders wrought
among the people; (and they were all with one accord
in Solomon's porch.)
—Acts 5:11–12

This was the greatest revival of the New Testament, greater in many ways than Pentecost. The disciples were all of one accord in one place, awaiting the outpouring of the Spirit. They all made the same sound. (See 2 Chronicles 5:13.) If you get to that place, God will shake the country.

Now, in this great revival, signs and wonders were effected, and *"none of the rest dared join them"* (Acts 5:13 NKJV). They were so full of fire that no one dared to say falsely, "I am one of you." They were afraid that God would strike them dead. God wants to get a people so full of power, His power, that others who are merely full of wildfire will not say, "God sent me."

The Holy Spirit

What was the result? Believers were added. To the church? No, *"to the Lord, multitudes of both men and women"* (v. 14). Some say that this excitement, this fanaticism, is well and good for women; however, there was a multitude of strong-minded men there.

"They brought forth the sick into the streets, and laid them on beds and couches, that at the least the shadow of Peter passing by might overshadow some of them" (v. 15). See what a "fanatical" lot they were! I wish we were just like that.

The excitement rose higher and higher. The whole country was stirred. A multitude came out of the cities around Jerusalem, bringing the sick, and they were all healed—every one (v. 16). They were healed because they came in the right way. This was a wonderful revival, was it not?

Yet the revival was broken up right in the middle of it. The high priest and Sadducees arrested the apostles and put them in prison. Bless God, they did not stay there long. God sent His angel down, brought them out of prison, and told them to go into the temple and preach to the people (vv. 17–20).

It took some grace to do that, did it not, to go right back there and preach all the Word, not leaving out divine healing, but showing all the signs and wonders? In the morning, the high priest and the others sent to have them brought out. They found the prison locked but no one there; those whom they sought were out preaching (vv. 21–25).

One Will Chase a Thousand

It is better to obey God than men (Acts 5:29). We are determined to obey God, whatever the result is.

The Great Revival in Jerusalem

God's people must meet persecution. People say that this work we are doing is not of God. That is the kind of talk the Devil likes to hear. All the Devil has to do is blow his whistle, and his army runs to do his work. God has to blow and blow on His whistle before He can get His people to do His work, yet we have the promise, *"One man of you shall chase a thousand"* (Josh. 23:10). The Devil hates holiness and power; he persecutes, and persecution is all that makes men fit for heaven.

This revival recorded in Acts 5 was a great revival. Every one of the apostles seemed to be there, and God gave them wonderful power. Many mighty signs and miracles were done by them because they were of one accord, preaching and believing. As a result of this, the fire of God fell upon the church, and sinners began to tremble.

I believe in preaching in such a way that the power of God will make people tremble—preaching holiness, coming up to the front to do His will. *"The fear of the LORD is the beginning of wisdom"* (Ps. 111:10). When we first know about God, a holy awe comes over us. When we want God to work, to cause His presence to be felt in our midst, we must believe He has the power to work among His people; it is a terrible thing to resist Him.

We must put on the full armor (Eph. 6:11) and rush into the battle. We must press the battle to the gates (Isa. 28:6). The help of man is vain. There is no shelter except in the wounded side of Jesus. It is the only place on earth to which we can flee. There we learn the way of righteousness; we know what awaits the sinner if he does not accept this shelter.

The Holy Spirit

God Confirms His Word

In the Old Testament, we read of God's workings among His people. When someone was sent with a message from God, it often seemed very foolish, humanly speaking. Yet what was the outcome? God will always show Himself and put His seal upon His work. When the message was delivered, He came forth with the supernatural, with the sign of His invisible presence.

He manifested His presence in miraculous ways. That put the fear of God upon the heathen. They said that there was no god like the God of the Hebrews, because of His wonderful works. He was a God to be feared.

In the New Testament, signs and wonders were done before the people. Wherever Jesus went, the people followed Him. God was with Him, putting the fear of God upon the people through the miracles, signs, and wonders that God worked through Him. Jesus said, "I do not do these things on my own. It is the Father who does the works." (See John 5:19; 14:10.) The apostles said the same: "By the mighty power of the Holy Spirit, Jesus does the works." (See Acts 2:32–33.) As the apostle Paul said: *"Not I, but Christ"* (Gal. 2:20).

It is the same today. In the signs and wonders that are occurring today, it is *"not I, but Christ."* He dwells within us, and the work is done by the mighty power of the Holy Spirit. *"Know ye not that your body is the temple of the Holy Ghost?"* (1 Cor. 6:19). Jesus Christ dwells in us. We are God's power plant.

It was by the hands of the apostles, not of angels, that God did His mighty works, and people believed when the signs followed (Mark 16:20). Jesus commanded the unclean spirits to come out, and they had to come. The power of the Holy Spirit went through the apostles' hands, and that is just the way God works today.

The apostles were not afraid of persecution, the sword, or anything else. They faced death in any form rather than disgrace the cause of Christ by being cowards. We serve a mighty God, and Jesus Christ who ascended into heaven is here by my side today. He will lead His hosts on to victory. Let us press the battle to the gates (Isa. 28:6).

This "sect" is always spoken against, misrepresented, and lied about (see Acts 28:22), but Jesus Christ is leading on His hosts. God permitted Jesus to be nailed to the cross and laid in the grave, but He came forth like the sun in the Resurrection. God permitted the apostles to be arrested and put in prison. Then He had an opportunity to show His power. He sent His angel and delivered them. The angel of the Lord is with His own. *"Our citizenship is in heaven"* (Phil. 3:20 NKJV). We are children of the King.

Around us, day and night, are ministering spirits, sent to minister to those who are heirs of salvation (Heb. 1:14). We can afford to be misrepresented or even put in prison, if we are only looking for the manifestation and the glory of translation, if we are only looking to go sweeping through the gates of heaven.

Persecution Comes When God Works

The apostles were persecuted, and the meeting was broken up in Jerusalem, where the Lord was crucified.

The Holy Spirit

The meeting was held in Solomon's porch, one of the prominent places in the city. It seems that the apostles were in this great porch; the sick were brought into the street on beds and couches, in every way, and placed all around—those who were sick, blind, and troubled by unclean spirits, a great multitude.

What would the preachers think if we brought the sick and placed them around the church in this way? In the first place (and in the second and third places, also), if they were preaching one of those fine sermons and someone dropped a sick person down in the middle of the congregation, they would send for a policeman quickly; you know they would.

In another New Testament incident, the paralytic did not break up the meeting when he was brought to Jesus and dropped down through the roof while the Lord was preaching. He is our example. Jesus was glad to have something like that happen, because it gave Him a chance to show His power. He forgave all of the man's sins and then made him rise, take up his bed, and walk. (See Mark 2:1–12.) The people began to shout "Glory" the same way you do here; you cannot help yourselves. If you have not done it, you will. A woman with tuberculosis was brought in here in her nightgown. I did not care what she had on; she was healed. Hallelujah!

When Jesus healed the paralytic, the people gave glory to God. People say today, "You never heard such a fanatical group!" If they had only heard the people giving glory to God then! We have something to make a fuss about. Dead people never make much noise, do they? There is not much noise in a graveyard. Some people are frozen; they're wearing grave clothes. May God take off our grave clothes and set us free!

The Great Revival in Jerusalem

David danced before the Lord with all his might. His wife Michal did not like it; she thought he had disgraced her before the handmaidens, and she began to grumble. He said he was not dancing before the handmaidens, but before the Lord. It is dangerous to meddle with a genuine work of the Lord. Michal had no child to the day of her death. (See 2 Samuel 6:14–23.) Barrenness was a great disappointment to a Jewish woman, as each one hoped to be the mother of the Lord.

Do not touch the work of the Lord. It meant sudden death to lay your hand upon the ark of the Lord. (See 2 Samuel 6:1–7.) Sometimes the Holy Spirit comes like a *"rushing mighty wind"* (Acts 2:2) from heaven and makes a great commotion among the people; other times, He comes silently. He comes to us here.

You need to take down your umbrellas and get your buckets right-side up. God will fill the vessels and make you a power plant for Him. Then God will show Himself mighty to pull down the strongholds of the Devil and build up the kingdom of Christ. (See 2 Corinthians 10:4–5.) You will have power to preach, and signs and wonders will be worked, as in the days of the apostles. The Lord was with them. He was invisible, but He was with them, confirming the Word with signs and wonders (Mark 16:20). He will never forsake us if we obey Him.

The Scripture says there were *"signs following"* (v. 20). Following what? The preaching of the Word. The Spirit of the Lord is here, and you will see Him with what we call "visible signs." Peter said, "What you see is the Holy Spirit." (See Acts 2:33.) If you are willing, you will see Him here, for God is coming in a wonderful way.

The Holy Spirit

At Pentecost, the people saw the fire on the apostles' heads and heard them speak in other tongues *"as the Spirit gave them utterance"* (Acts 2:4); they saw them stagger like drunken men. Wherever the Holy Spirit is poured out, you will see signs.

The Power of the Holy Spirit

Returning to our text, that revival in Jerusalem was a great meeting. The sick were brought on beds and cots, and God, through the apostles, worked many signs and wonders. The fear of God fell on the people. Thousands and thousands were converted to God. Their names were written in heaven. They were filled with the Holy Spirit, the glory of God; the power of God was great. Not all the sick could get close enough to have hands laid on them for healing. Peter seemed to be the leader in this divine healing movement, and they tried to get the sick near enough so that Peter's shadow might fall on some of them. Pentecost filled the apostles, and people were healed even watching for Peter's shadow.

The power was of the Holy Spirit. He who believes in Jesus Christ will have such power that out of his inward parts will flow *"rivers of living water"* (John 7:38). The Holy Spirit is like a river. The power of the Holy Spirit struck the sick ones and healed them, and the people marveled. Jesus Himself did many mighty works, and He told the apostles that they would do even greater things if they believed in Him (John 14:12).

Men and women, God wants you to get into that place. Don't you see that God works through human instrumentality? God will use us if we are swallowed up in Him. In our meetings in Chicago, people were healed sitting in their seats, and away up in the gallery, some fell completely under the power of God.

The power of God is going out while I am talking. You know I am speaking the truth; believe it, accept it, and get more of Jesus. If we take in and take in and do not give out, we are like a sponge that needs to be squeezed. Let us get so full that it will run right out through us, and not absorb and absorb, and never give out.

Many of you are baptized with the Holy Spirit. You ought to send the power toward me while I send it toward you, and when the two come together, something will happen. I could not stay on my feet if you would do this. Glory! Glory to God!

Get a clear picture of that revival in Jerusalem. Did they act like crazy folks? Some of the best people in Jerusalem took part in that revival. All classes of people were there. They were under the power of the Spirit, getting healed, or running to bring someone else to be healed. Multitudes were saved.

Healing the Sick Is Part of the Gospel

It was the greatest revival, and divine healing was the drawing card. When people are healed, the end result is not just healing; people are also brought to faith in Christ. The account of the man healed at the Beautiful Gate of the temple is an example of this. Peter took the miracle of healing as his text, and he preached to the people. Then the authorities apprehended Peter and John and commanded them not to speak or teach in the name of Jesus. But Peter and John said that they

The Holy Spirit

would preach in His name anyway. They prayed, and the Holy Spirit came in great power. The outgrowth of that healing in the temple was a wonderful revival. (See Acts 3:10–4:4.)

Returning to the great revival in Jerusalem, notice the mighty power that went from Peter's body. His very shadow healed people. Paul also did special miracles; handkerchiefs and aprons that he had touched were sent out, and the people were healed through them. This is different from any other miracle in the New Testament, but God is doing the same thing today.

The Holy Spirit works through our hands, through our bodies! We are sending out thousands of handkerchiefs all over the country, over land and sea. I could tell you wonderful stories of the work they do; five were healed from one handkerchief.

As we lift up Jesus, God sends His power through us, as He did in apostolic days. Let us rise and shine and give God the glory.

When I first started out to preach, I did not know I was to pray for anyone to be healed, but God showed me I was to preach divine healing. The Devil tried to hold me back, but thousands have been healed and saved since.

I lay hands on the sick in the name of Jesus. It is Jesus who makes us whole. Sometimes the power is so great that people are healed instantly, leaping and jumping and praising God. The Lord is here; we can have as great a revival as they had in Jerusalem, and the fear of God will be upon the people.

God wants you to march to the Cross and give glory to God. We need to get to work here. Let Him do the work in your soul first. We are going to have a revival here like the one in Jerusalem, with many signs and wonders.

Getting divine healing isn't like going to the doctor. Get baptized with the Holy Spirit before you leave; then, when you get home, you will not backslide. Glory to God!

Chapter 11

The Fire and Glory
Filling the Temple

*The house was filled with a cloud, even the house
of the LORD; so that the priests could not stand to
minister by reason of the cloud: for the glory of the
LORD had filled the house of God.*
—2 Chronicles 5:13–14

It came to pass, when the priests were come out of the
holy place" (2 Chron. 5:11). I want you to see how
they came: one hundred and twenty of them with
different instruments, yet all making the same sound.
The Levites were arrayed in white linen, emblematic of
purity.

> *It came even to pass, as the trumpeters and singers
> were as one, to make one sound to be heard in prais-
> ing and thanking the LORD; and…they lifted up their
> voice with the trumpets and cymbals and instruments
> of music, and praised the LORD.* (v. 13)

The Holy Spirit

There were one hundred and twenty priests blowing trumpets; there were singers and instruments of music; but they *"were as one, to make one sound."* They praised God, saying, *"For he is good; for his mercy endureth for ever"* (v. 13).

> *The house was filled with a cloud, even the house of the LORD; so that the priests could not stand to minister by reason of the cloud: for the glory of the LORD had filled the house of God.*

The one hundred and twenty priests who were supposed to minister stood like statues, and the Holy Spirit took over the meeting. The entire building was filled with the glory of God.

All this demonstration, the house being filled with the glory of God, was brought about by the one hundred and twenty priests blowing the trumpets. The playing of the different instruments was mingled with the voices of the great company of singers. The whole object was to glorify God, with everyone making one sound.

God wants perfect harmony. He doesn't want anyone criticizing or finding fault; He wants everyone sounding forth His praise, in purity. If we go out to meet God clothed in white, washed in the blood of the Lamb; if we go out, all making the same sound; if we go out to glorify God, God will honor all the noise.

It is not just excitement. God Himself comes down to acknowledge the praise. They praised and honored God, and the power of God came down. That same power will either save or destroy us someday. The house of God was filled with the power and glory of the Lord.

The Fire and Glory Filling the Temple

Living Temples Praise God

There was no preaching then, but singing, shouting, and praising the Lord, and all who praised glorified God. The house was filled with His glory. The people were standing, and Solomon was ready to dedicate the temple. The temple represents the church of Jesus; it also represents our bodies. *"Know ye not that your body is the temple of the* [living God]*?"* (1 Cor. 6:19).

What happens in 2 Chronicles 7:1–3 is like Pentecost; it represents Pentecost. The first verse reads, *"When Solomon had made an end of praying."* So many people never look to God to answer their prayers; they would be frightened if He did. Solomon stretched out His hands and prayed to God, and God heard him.

When he had finished praying, something happened. God will come forth if you are not afraid of the power, if you are ready to stand for God with everything that is within you. As Pentecostal people, we should always be "prayed up," so that we can get hold of God quickly and be sure it is for the glory of God.

"The fire came down from heaven, and consumed the burnt offering and the sacrifices; and the glory of the LORD filled the house" (2 Chron. 7:1). Some people talk as if God never had any glory, as though the glory of God was never seen at any time.

The apostle Paul wrote,

If the ministration [ministry] *of death, written and engraven in stones, was glorious, so that the children of Israel could not stedfastly behold the face of Moses for the glory of his countenance; which glory was to be*

done away: how shall not the ministration [ministry]
of the spirit be rather glorious?   (2 Cor. 3:7–8)

The glory under the law did not last; but the Holy
Spirit came at Pentecost to stay. The manifestations
under the ministry of the Holy Spirit are to be with much
greater glory; they are to exceed in glory. The power
under the law was only a shadow of what we ought to have
under grace. This was the ministry of life, not death.

I am glad that the glory of God has been seen here
a number of times. Many times in our ministry, the
glory of God has been seen over us. God is here. This
is what you see and hear (Acts 2:33). *"This is that which
was spoken by the prophet Joel"* (v. 16). This is the promise
of the Father; this is the Holy Spirit.

As I said earlier, when Solomon had finished praying, the house of the Lord was filled with God's glory.
The people saw and felt it; it was not a shadow. The
priests could not enter into the house; they could not
get in at all, because the glory of the Lord had filled the
Lord's house.

*When all the children of Israel saw how the fire came
down, and the glory of the LORD upon the house, they
bowed themselves with their faces to the ground upon
the pavement, and worshipped, and praised the LORD,
saying, For he is good; for his mercy endureth for ever.*
(2 Chron. 7:3)

Everything connected with this represents our present glorious age. The apostle Paul said that God can
reveal His doctrine, which has been hidden for all ages
(Col. 1:26). Those who crucified the Lord did not know
about the mystical body of Christ. They did not know

the divine life we have received, or they would not have crucified Him. It could be revealed only when the Holy Spirit came down from God to make men understand the new covenant.

The glory that belonged to the *"ministration of death"* (2 Cor. 3:7) did not come to stay. The glory came from the ark of the covenant, which contained the tablets of stone on which the law was written, the Ten Commandments. On the mercy seat of the ark of the covenant, there were the cherubim, two golden angels, facing each other, with wings outspread over the mercy seat, where God dwells in His temple. In His tabernacle—that is, in us, who are the temples of the Holy Spirit (1 Cor. 6:19)—nothing is supposed to be in the heart but God's Word, the new and everlasting covenant. It is written on the tablets of the heart, not on stone, by the finger of God Almighty (2 Cor. 3:3).

We May Always Be Filled with God's Glory

If, when the Old Testament people obeyed, the glory of God came down and the people fell prostrate, how much glory ought there to be today? Then there was just one tabernacle and two tablets of stone. Today your body is the temple of the living God. Our bodies are the temples of the Holy Spirit, and God writes His Word in our hearts with His own finger.

The ancient temple in all its glory represents each one of our bodies. If we are filled with the Holy Spirit as we ought to be, our bodies will be flooded with *"rivers of living water"* (John 7:38) that flow out to others.

We will also be on fire for God. The glory of the Lord was seen over the ark. Inside the tabernacle, the lamp was always burning. Since it was kept supplied with oil, it never went out. In the temple that is each of our bodies, God puts His love in our hearts. He wants us to keep the light always burning and never let it go out. By keeping all obstructions out of the channel of faith, we get a supply of oil continually; the light will always shine through the tabernacle. If the oracle written on stone was glorious, how much more glorious is the ministry of the Spirit under grace! The Holy Spirit will abide with us always.

Jesus said that if we keep His commandments, He and the Father will both take up their abode with us (John 14:23). They will dwell with us, and we will be flooded with the Holy Spirit. We are a people to be wondered at. Jesus said, "Here am I, and the children You have given me." (See John 17:9–11, 24.)

There should be perfect fellowship and harmony among believers; we should all make *"one sound"* (2 Chron. 5:13). The glory came down at Solomon's prayer. At a glimpse of that glory, they lost their strength, and the whole multitude bowed down to the ground and worshipped God.

When we are praying for people to get saved or healed, some shout, some praise, some pray, but all are making the same sound. We put on the blood of Jesus by faith and get a glimpse of His glory. Is it any wonder that people lose their strength and fall prostrate under the new life that comes to them? Is it strange that we are people to be wondered at? You have seen all this here: singing, playing, making the same sound. Is it any wonder that these people who come here especially to get under the blood as never before fall prostrate when they get a glimpse of Jesus?

You must prove that God has changed, that He has taken His power away, before you condemn us. *"The gifts and the calling of God are irrevocable"* (Rom. 11:29 NKJV). He never changes. He is the same yesterday, today, and forever (Heb. 13:8).

No one has any right to condemn us, to say that the people are hypnotized or crazy or have lost their minds or that I have put a spell on them. Great God, awaken the people before the thunders of Judgment rouse them! You must throw the Bible away, or you must prove that the gifts and callings have been taken from the church, before you reject us.

We are going the Bible route, and you have no business teaching anything else; you must stick to the Word of God. We do not hold anything up but the Word of God. It is good enough for me. *"I am not ashamed of the gospel of Christ"* (Rom. 1:16) or of His power.

What a wonderful people we are in our privileges! Today, every believer may be God's priest (Rev. 1:6). If we abide in Him, and His words abide in us, we may ask what we will, and it will be done (John 15:7). We indeed have wonderful privileges. The power of the Lord shines forth a hundred times greater than under the law; the power then was typical of Pentecost.

Get your Bibles and search out these things; you are getting the light of God, and He expects you to *"walk in the light"* (1 John 1:7), even if you get it from a little weak woman like me. In His name, I tell you these things are true. What do you care about man's opinion when you are standing before God? Dried opinions and the traditions of men all go to destruction, but it is the living Word that I am preaching to you.

The Signs of the Holy Spirit

When John the Baptist was in prison, he began to doubt a little whether Jesus was the Christ, and he sent his disciples to ask Him, *"Art thou he that should come, or do we look for another?"* (Matt. 11:3). Jesus did not say, "I belong to the church" or "I belong to a college." He said, "Go and tell John the things you have seen here: the lame walk, the blind see, different diseases are healed, and the poor have the Gospel preached to them. Blessed is he who will not be offended because of Me." (See verses 4–6.) Men get mad at the signs of the Holy Spirit. They get jealous; they spit out hatred; they are trying to tear down God's work.

If John did not believe in Christ through the signs, no eloquence would be of value. If he did not believe what the witnesses told him, he would not believe anything, and neither will you! There is the genuine, and there is the Devil's counterfeit, as surely as you live.

If all you do is stand back and watch, it will seem like foolishness to you as we praise God and as people get filled with the Holy Spirit and receive gifts. But it is Jesus first, last, and all the time. We lift up Jesus and praise His name. We see bright, happy faces; we see pain go out of bodies. We go home rejoicing, feeling as if we have heaven here below.

Resist the Devil in the name of the Lord. Sometimes, when I am standing up preaching, the Devil tries to interfere. He would make me drop dead, if I would listen to him. I resist in the name of the Lord, and he has to go. (See James 4:7.) We have such a wonderful Savior!

The Scripture says, *"[You] shall lay hands on the sick"* (Mark 16:18). God commissioned me, and I obey God rather than man (Acts 5:29). Neither the deadly serpent nor any poison will harm you. You will cast out devils. (See Mark 16:17–18.) I believe every bit of it, and I have seen it all. Hallelujah!

I got my commission from the Lord, and I did not go until He called me and until I was baptized and qualified. I get my message from heaven. I do not know what I am going to talk about, but God knows everyone here and just what everyone needs, and He will give you something.

Power for Service

The power that Jesus promised His disciples when He told them to wait at Jerusalem was to change their lives and qualify them to transact the business of heaven. When they were baptized with the Holy Spirit, they would be true to their Master and be witnesses for Him. Therefore, after the disciples watched Jesus ascend into heaven, they went down from the mountain praising the Lord. They were filled with a great joy as they went back to Jerusalem to await the fulfillment of the promise. They had confidence in God. He had said it would happen, and they began to praise Him in anticipation.

Are you full of joy, with no doubts that Jesus is your Lord and Savior? You need power to do the work of God; you need to be clothed with power. God says He will baptize you with fire, bestowing on you wisdom, knowledge, and gifts. He will cause you to understand the *"deep things of God"* (1 Cor. 2:10). As you teach them and live them, God will be with you.

Be of One Accord

You must believe that you are going to receive this blessing. The disciples were *"with one accord"* (Acts 1:14). May God help us to get to that place. God wants us of one accord, our hearts running together like drops of water.

A little company of believers like that could shake a city in a day. We are not of one accord when one is pulling this way and another is pulling that way—when we hear "maybe this" and "maybe that." Do you suppose God will bless you in that?

You cannot understand the first principles. Yet once you have the newborn joy in your heart, when you see it in someone else, you will know it is of God. Be of one mind; no matter how much there is to praise God for, we always want more.

At Pentecost, the disciples suddenly heard a sound like a mighty, rushing wind (Acts 2:2). This Holy Spirit we are holding up is a mighty power. He came from heaven like a windstorm, like floods of water filling up vessels, like fire upon the heads of one hundred and twenty people.

"Cloven tongues…of fire" (v. 3), as it were, sat upon the disciples' heads. Then the Holy Spirit went in and took possession of the temple, took full possession of the machinery, wound it up, and set it running for God. They staggered and fell like drunken people. This mighty power took possession of their tongues and spoke through them in other languages.

The Fire and Glory Filling the Temple

Way back in the time of the prophets, it was said, *"With stammering lips and another tongue will he speak to this people"* (Isa. 28:11). Think of that! God doing such a mighty thing! But some do not want to believe. That is the way the Holy Spirit came, and that is the way He comes today. Yet people say it is some other power.

The disciples had not lost their minds; they had just found them! They had received the spirit of love and a sound mind (2 Tim. 1:7). We never have sound minds until we receive the mind of Christ. People who cannot understand this say that these things are foolishness. We are told that the *"wisdom of this world is foolishness with God"* (1 Cor. 3:19). This is the power of God and the wisdom of God, not the work of the Devil—people saying so doesn't make it so.

God had complete control. He came in and took possession of the disciples at Pentecost. Now, the Holy Spirit is in the world today. If you disagree, you must first prove that He has been taken away, as well as the gifts and callings, before you have a right to lay hands on God's people.

The things called foolishness today are the *"power of God unto salvation"* (Rom. 1:16). Step out into the deep with God. Paul told us that the Lord ascended into heaven and sent down gifts *"for the perfecting of the saints, for the work of the ministry, for the edifying of the body of Christ"* (Eph. 4:12; see also verses 7–8, 11).

God's Children Built Up in Christ

The ministry does not lack the gifts today. Saints, that is, Christians, are baptized with the Holy Spirit so that the whole body may be edified, no matter how much a believer has already received. When God is working, every one of His children is edified. If God works through someone else, I am edified and encouraged, and I rejoice.

The working of the Holy Spirit is the visible sign of the presence of Jesus. The disciples went from Jerusalem to preach the Gospel everywhere, and the Lord *"was with them"* (Acts 11:21; see Mark 16:20). I love that truth. Is He in heaven? Yes, but He is with us also.

The Lord was with them, *"confirming the word"* (Mark 16:20). How? *"With signs* [and wonders] *following"* (v. 20). Wherever they went, they saw faces shine, someone healed, someone speaking in tongues. What you *"now see and hear"* is of the Holy Spirit (Acts 2:33), and it is for the work of the ministry.

If I did not know that Jesus is by my side with His loving arms around me, I could not stand here today. I would not have the strength if I did not know that He dwells in this body. If I did not know by experience that these things are true, I could not stand here.

I have tested the truth; I know it is of God. How can we help talking of the things we have seen? (See Acts 4:20.) I have seen things by the Spirit and in visions. I have seen Jesus, the heavens open, the Marriage Supper, hosts of angels, the glory of God. I have seen them, glory to God! I know what I am telling you. I know that Jesus lives and is standing by my side, more truly than I know you are here. These things are verities.

"I am not ashamed of the gospel of Christ" (Rom. 1:16). Glory to God! When a weak woman comes here to tell you what strong men ought to have told you, what are you going to think about it? I say that these things are

true. When people say they are foolishness and fanaticism, do they dare to attempt to prove it by the Word? I dare them to do it.

When they can prove that the Holy Spirit has been taken out of the world, away from God's people, I am ready to go to prison, but not before.

Chapter 12

The Former and the Latter Rain

The Lord is in our midst. Be still and know the voice of God: *"The LORD is in his holy temple: let all the earth keep silence before him"* (Hab. 2:20). Let us try to realize His wonderful presence. We must all meet Him sooner or later as individuals; it is a good thing to get acquainted with Him now.

This Scripture applies to us today:

> *It shall come to pass in the last days, saith God, I will pour out of my Spirit upon all flesh: and your sons and your daughters shall prophesy, and your young men shall see visions, and your old men shall dream dreams: and on my servants and on my handmaidens I will pour out in those days of my Spirit; and they shall prophesy: and I will show wonders in heaven above, and signs in the earth beneath; blood, and fire, and vapour of smoke: the sun shall be turned into darkness, and the moon into blood, before that great and notable day of the Lord come.*
>
> (Acts 2:17–20, quoting Joel 2:28–31)

The Holy Spirit

This is a wonderful Scripture, and many do not understand it. There is a certain time spoken of here, when certain great and wonderful things will take place and people will know that prophecy is being fulfilled. *"It shall come to pass in the last days, saith God, I will pour out of my Spirit upon all flesh"* (Acts 2:17). There will be signs in the heavens and the earth—signs of His coming. The Holy Spirit will be poured out before the *"notable day of the Lord come*[s]*"* (v. 20).

This prophecy was first spoken eight hundred years before Jesus came to earth. Peter, standing up on the Day of Pentecost, recited the prophecy and confirmed it. Under the inspiration of the Holy Spirit, on fire with the Holy Spirit from head to foot, speaking with a tongue of fire, he said that these things would come to pass in the last days.

We Are in the Last Days

We believe and know by the Word of God and by the signs that we are now living in the last days, the very times Peter spoke about, which we were to know by the mighty things taking place. We are the people, and this is the time, just before the *"notable day of the Lord"* bursts upon the world. We believe we are the people; yes, we know it. We have a right to our belief, for it is based upon the Word of God, and no man or woman has any right to denounce our teaching or to injure us in any way until it can be proved by the Word of God that the things we teach are not true.

You should give us a hearing. Then take the same Word of God and prove by it that the things we teach are not true—if you can. You must first prove that the Holy Spirit, working in all His mighty miraculous power, has been done away with before you have any right to denounce us as frauds and hypocrites on account of these things that we say come from God.

As I wrote earlier, whenever anyone, minister or lawyer, can take the platform and prove by the Word of God that the Holy Spirit and His mighty, miraculous power have been taken away from the church, I am willing to go to prison, but not before. It cannot be done. God never recalls His gifts (Rom. 11:29). God never changes. My Bible says, *"Jesus Christ the same yesterday, and to day, and for ever"* (Heb. 13:8).

There are many ways besides the working of the Holy Spirit by which we know we are in the last days. Joel, in speaking of the last days, tells us many things I don't have time to mention today, which show us that we are in this time. Nahum tells us that when this time comes, it will be the *"day of his preparation"* (Nah. 2:3). God is preparing men so that they may be taken out of the world before the Tribulation comes.

Before the flood, Noah was commanded by God to build an ark. It took him just five years to build the ark—though many believe it was much longer than that—and the time he was building it was the preparation time in those days. Noah, at God's command, was preparing a place for himself and his family where they would be in safety, above the storm that was coming, above the waves and billows. At the same time that the old world was getting a warning, Noah was building the ark.

Signs of the Last Days

Jesus compared that day of preparation to our time in these last days. (See Matthew 24:37–44.) It is a short period and has been going on for some time already. It is prophesied that there will be great signs in the earth: blood, fire, smoke, earthquakes, great destruction. All these things have been coming upon the earth in the last few years. God has a time for everything. The book of Daniel says that in the *"time of the end: many shall run to and fro, and knowledge shall be increased"* (Dan. 12:4). Nahum said, *"The chariots shall rage in the streets, they shall justle one against another in the broad ways: they shall seem like torches, they shall run like the lightnings"* (Nah. 2:4).

Jesus sent the Holy Spirit with mighty signs and wonders. He took possession of men, and they staggered like drunken men; they were drunk but not with wine. They spoke with *"stammering lips and another tongue"* (Isa. 28:11). These things happened when Pentecost first came, in order to establish the church in power. That was the early rain (James 5:7).

In the last days, the time of preparation, God will cause the early rain to come again as at Pentecost, and He will also give the *"latter rain"* (v. 7) abundantly in the same month. What do you think of that? The early disciples went to heaven by the death route. It will take a double portion of the Spirit to fill our bodies, to make us sound in spirit, soul, and body. When Jesus comes like a flash of lightning (Matt. 24:27), He will change these bodies of ours in a moment, and they will be made like His glorious body (Phil. 3:21).

"Behold, I show you a mystery; we shall not all sleep, but we shall all be changed" (1 Cor. 15:51) and will rise *"to meet the Lord in the air"* (1 Thess. 4:17). When are these things to be? At the end of the day of preparation, just before the Tribulation bursts upon the world. We are to watch for the signs and not forsake the *"assembling of*

ourselves together" (Heb. 10:25)—and so much the more as we see the Day of the Lord approaching! Glory to God!

The Jews understood something about heeding the warnings of God. They said one to another, "We have been wounded; we have gone through many troubles; let us turn to the Lord. (See Lamentations 3:1–40.) *'After two days will he revive us: in the third day he will raise us up'* (Hos. 6:2)."

We are now down to the end of the second thousand years since Christ set up His kingdom. Now, what will happen to the Jews? The Jews today have great liberty in Palestine, so much so that they are going back by the thousands and building up the waste places. Modern improvements are there today, and they are hoping for something, but they do not know what. After the Tribulation, the Jews will return to the Lord.

The Holy Spirit was first poured out at Pentecost. *"In the last days...I will pour out of my Spirit upon all flesh"* (Acts 2:17). The prophecy does not say that He will sprinkle a few drops, but *"pour out...upon all flesh"*—a cloudburst! This will happen just at the end; it will continue until the saints are taken away. Then the Tribulation will burst upon the earth. Some of the signs will be, *"Your sons and your daughters shall prophesy"* (v. 17). It is very plain so that everyone may understand. There is to be a wonderful ministry in the last days. Paul said that male and female are one in Christ (Gal. 3:28). Both will prophesy in the last days. That is the effect of the outpouring of the Holy Spirit. Other signs will be the following: devils will be cast out; hands will be laid on the sick, and they will recover; many will speak with new tongues; if anyone drinks poison accidentally, it will not hurt him; and serpents will not be able to harm believers. (See Mark 16:17–18.)

The Bride Is Almost Ready

See the power that has been given to man today: he has even chained the lightning. It is the day for preparation. Men *"run to and fro"* (Dan. 12:4) and fly over the land. Hurry up! The ark will soon be finished, and then God will say, "Come up." The ark went up above the waters; the world went down. God is preparing His spiritual ark today. The body of Christ will soon be complete, and when it is complete, it will go above the treetops to meet our Lord and King in the air (1 Thess. 4:17). We are in the day of preparation of the King of Glory, and His bride is making herself ready (Rev. 19:7). Rejoice and be glad, for the Marriage of the Lamb is at hand. The bride must be arrayed in white linen, the robe of righteousness, clothed in the power of the mighty God through His outpoured Spirit.

She is getting her garments ready to meet the Bridegroom. I praise the Lord that I am living in this day. The bride will be caught up just before the Tribulation bursts upon this sin-cursed earth. The bride must be very beautiful. She is represented as a queen dressed in a robe of finest needlework (Ps. 45:13–14). What is that fine wedding dress, the garments the bride will wear when she meets the Lord in the air? She will shine with the gifts and jewels of the Holy Spirit. *"We have this treasure in earthen vessels"* (2 Cor. 4:7), but they who are wise will shine as the brightness of the sun (Dan. 12:3). The wise will know when these things are coming, when the ark is about ready to go up. (See Daniel 2:21–22; 12:10.)

The Former and the Latter Rain

The Lord will not keep any secrets from them. As there is perfect confidence between bride and Bridegroom, so Jesus will reveal secrets to His bride. He will show us the *"deep things of God"* (1 Cor. 2:10), and we will know when the end is drawing near. You must make your own wedding garments; you cannot hire someone to make them. The time is coming. People do not usually begin to make wedding garments until the wedding day is near.

A bride is very happy, is willing to forsake her father's house, her friends, everything, and go with her bridegroom, even to a foreign country. She loves those she leaves, but he is dearer to her than anything else. We must be willing to leave anything and everything to go with Jesus. The bride of Christ will be taken out from among men, and many men and women will be left behind. You may say, "I do not believe it." I believe it!

Do you suppose that I would leave my home, my friends, and the only child that I have, to spend my life for others, if I did not know these things were so? God has revealed these things by His Word and by signs, and I know they are true. God is almighty. He is putting His seal upon this truth every day; He is putting the seal of the Holy Spirit upon people every day. The Holy Spirit is a witness to you, by mighty signs and wonders, that we are preaching the Word of God. I call God to witness that the Holy Spirit is putting His seal upon the work here. There are signs here every day. What are you going to do about it? If you believe the Bible, you must accept it. We have the eternal Word to stand on, and stronger is He who is with us than all that can be against us. (See 1 John 4:4.)

The Holy Spirit

Signs Follow the Word

After Pentecost, the disciples went out and preached the Holy Spirit sent by the ascended Jesus, and He confirmed the Word *"with signs following"* (Mark 16:20). I say before God that He is confirming the Word here every day, and these miracles are written down in heaven's record. Jesus Christ is the Healer and the Baptizer. John the Baptist said, *"He that cometh after me is mightier than I…he shall baptize you with the Holy Ghost, and with fire"* (Matt. 3:11). I praise God that some of the fire has struck this place. You can make flowery speeches, and the Devil will just laugh, but this work stirs the Devil. It is *"by my spirit, saith the LORD"* (Zech. 4:6).

Paul said that his teaching was *"not with enticing words of man's wisdom, but in demonstration of the Spirit and of power"* (1 Cor. 2:4). That shook the world, and it is just the same today. You say, "I do not like this power." Well, the Devil does not like it, either. I have been ministering for thirty-five years, and people fell under the power of God by the thousands before I preached healing. There were mighty outpourings of the Spirit that made the Devil howl. It shows how little we know of the real Gospel when we take the letter of the law (see Romans 7:6); it is like skimmed milk.

No man can understand the *"deep things of God"* (1 Cor. 2:10) except by the Spirit. Paul had much knowledge, but He said that the wisdom of this world is foolishness in the sight of God (3:19). True wisdom comes from heaven. The Word must be preached in simplicity. Jesus had the eloquence of high heaven at His command, yet He used language that the most uneducated could understand.

The Former and the Latter Rain

Preach in a simple way and demonstrate. The seal is put upon the Word by the Holy Spirit. Many people say that when we lay hands upon people, they get mesmerized. I am sorry that they do not know more of the power of God.

The Bible tells us that there was a great revival in Samaria through Philip's ministry. Simon the sorcerer and many others had been baptized in water in the name of the Lord Jesus, but none of the believers there had been baptized with the Holy Spirit. Then Peter and John went to Samaria and laid their hands on the new Christians, and they received the Holy Spirit. The Spirit was imparted to them in some way through the laying on of the apostles' hands. Simon recognized that the power was different from sorcery, and he wanted it. He offered the apostles money in exchange for this power, so that whoever he laid hands on might receive the Holy Spirit. (See Acts 8:5–19.)

The apostles were horrified. Peter said, *"Thy money perish with thee, because thou hast thought that the gift of God may be purchased with money"* (v. 20). The Holy Spirit and His power are gifts of God; you cannot buy them. Many people today do not understand that any more than Simon did. The apostles told him to repent, or he would be lost: *"Repent therefore of this your wickedness, and pray God if perhaps the thought of your heart may be forgiven you. For I see that you are poisoned by bitterness and bound by iniquity"* (vv. 22–23 NKJV). May God open the eyes of the people!

The Workings of the Spirit

Something happened by the laying on of the apostles' hands. The Holy Spirit fell on those people, and they had great blessing. There were great demonstrations in those days when the Holy Spirit fell on the people. The thought is that when hands were laid on people, something happened: they spoke in other languages, their mouths were filled with laughter, and sometimes they fell prostrate like dead men.

You must prove that God has taken this power away before you judge us harshly. Peter told the multitude that the things they saw on the Day of Pentecost were the things the prophets had said would come. (See Acts 2:14–36.) You may ask why people fall down in our meetings. What is our little strength under the power of God? Whenever people get a glimpse of God's glory, they lose their strength and fall.

The Impact of God's Glory

When Paul described the vision he had received from God, he said he did not know whether he had been in the body or out of the body at that time, but that God knew. (See 2 Corinthians 12:1–4.) When John the Revelator saw the glory of God in a vision, he fell *"as* [one] *dead"* (Rev. 1:17). When Daniel had a vision, he fell on his face; then a hand touched him and placed him on his hands and knees—you have never seen anything like that—and he was taken up, strengthened, and saw a great vision. The men who were with Daniel fled, so they did not see the vision. Daniel did not flee; he saw it, but he fell prostrate. (See Daniel 10:1–12:13.) When we experience just a little manifestation of God's power, we lose our strength and fall down.

Some of you do not understand the working of the Spirit. You are not near enough to God to know that it is the work of the Spirit.

The Former and the Latter Rain

Peter was on the housetop, praying, and he lost his strength and went down. A voice from heaven called him three times. (See Acts 10:9–16.) Sometimes, God teaches us more in ten minutes when we are lost to this world than we would otherwise learn in months. Paul, as he journeyed to Damascus persecuting the Christians, was struck down to the earth when the light shone from heaven, and those who were with him also fell to the earth. Paul said that the light was brighter than the sun, yet this happened at midday when the sun was at its strength. All those men fell from their horses and rolled in the dust when the glory of God passed by. Paul was struck blind and was blind for three days. (See Acts 9:1–9.)

When Jesus went to the grave, He went down as a corpse. But when He rose from the dead, the soldiers fell down at the manifestation of God's power and glory. (See Matthew 28:1–4.)

You must prove that God no longer manifests His power and glory before you condemn us. Remember the first martyr, Stephen. He was a man full of faith, wisdom, and power; he was full of the Holy Spirit (Acts 6:5, 8). Learned men tried to confound him, but they could not do it; then they were jealous and wanted to get rid of him. They hired men of the baser sort—that is the kind for that work—who lied about this mighty servant of God.

They arrested Stephen, and there he was before the great assembly. He did not try to defend himself, but he took the opportunity offered to preach to them about Jesus. He was filled with the Holy Spirit. His face was as the face of an angel, and those who bore false testimony against him, so that he lost his life, saw it. He did not look like a liar and a hypocrite. He was a servant of Almighty God.

The Holy Spirit

You can sometimes see that light today in the faces of God's children. Stephen looked up into heaven and saw the glory of God. He saw Jesus who had risen from the dead, standing at the right hand of God, and he told the people about it. (Oh, Lord, open the eyes of these people, and let them see the angels of the Lord encamped around us and Jesus standing in the midst!)

When Stephen told what he saw, they gnashed their teeth; they did not intend to repent. They dragged him out and stoned him to death, but the Lord permitted it and received him. God promises that His people will be protected, and when trouble comes, it is not a sign that He has forsaken them. Stephen's enemies did not like the fact that God received him, nor did they like to see his face shine with the glory of God. His body was lying as a bruised mass, but his spirit rose to meet the Lord. He had a glorious vision. (See Acts 6:8–7:60.) Do you believe he saw the throne of God and Jesus standing there? People talk about these things as though they were fables.

The Signs of the Times

God says that before Jesus comes, these signs and wonders will come to pass: the sick will be healed, devils will be cast out, and people will speak with tongues. (See Mark 16:17–18.) I am so glad for these days. When Jesus came the first time, He rebuked the Jewish leaders. He told them they could discern the face of the sky but not the signs of the times (Matt. 16:3). *"How is it that ye do not discern this time?"* (Luke 12:56). How much more will Jesus upbraid people when He returns? "Why didn't you see the signs? Why didn't you listen to My messengers? Why didn't you look at the Word and see whether they were telling the truth or were impostors?" Excuses won't do when we stand before Jesus. The light has come. Let us rise and shine and give God the glory!

Nothing but the mighty Holy Spirit will ever take you up in the clouds. He will quicken these mortal bodies (Rom. 8:11), and they will be changed. Christ rose from the dead, and He is the *"resurrection, and the life"* (John 11:25). We will know the power of the resurrection life. We will be so filled with the Holy Spirit that our bodies will be made light. We will not have wings, but our hands and feet will be made light. Our feet will be like *"hinds' feet"* (2 Sam. 22:34) as we run, skip, and almost fly. Sometimes my body is made so light, I can hardly stay. My feet are on the earth, but my hands seem to be near the throne.

People need to have the blood of Jesus covering them, covering their diseased bodies in His name. Do you believe right now? If you believe so that you praise the Lord in faith, it will be done. If you do not feel the joy, offer praise as a sacrifice, and ask God to give you the joy. When the unclean spirit is driven out, the disease goes, and the resurrection life comes in. Then you lose the small amount of human strength that you have, and you go down like Daniel, John, and the rest of them, and you lie down in green pastures.

Some people dance, shout, and praise the Lord as the life of Jesus thrills through them. I declare to you on the authority of God and from my own experience, I know that this is the power of God through Jesus Christ. It does not take Jesus long to do the work, but it takes some of us a long time to get there. Five minutes will do the work. Then the peace of God will flow through you like a river, and you will have joy in the

Holy Spirit. As you go home, don't think about your sins; don't commit any more, and don't worry about the past—it is under the blood.

God gave me a message, and He has given me the strength to stand here and deliver it. He asks you in a loving way to meet the Lord in the air, to attend the Marriage Supper. Will you meet me there? He is coming so soon. I often think that I will live until He comes.

I praise Him today that I know these things about the Holy Spirit. Sometimes people get into the flesh and make too much of a demonstration, but that is better than never to talk, pray, or sing. Let us not condemn, but let us all try to get nearer to God. That is what I am striving for today.

Oh, God, I have held up your Son today. I have honored His name with all the strength you have given me. Take the scales off the eyes of those who do not see, and cause them to see the truths that have been brought out! May they think of them again and again, and may they go to You to find out whether these things are so. You know how I have pleaded with people not to lay hands on the ark of the covenant or on the Lord's anointed. Open the eyes of those who have known only dead formality, and cause them to know that I am Your servant. Lord, I want the joy bells to ring in heaven because they are on the way, but you cannot take them against their will. I pray that I may meet them at the Marriage Supper of the Lamb.

Chapter 13

The Blood and Fire Mark

Today, the same things are taking place that took place at the time of the destruction of Jerusalem. Nearly twenty-six hundred years ago, the Lord gave the prophet Ezekiel this vision:

He cried also in mine ears with a loud voice, saying, Cause them that have charge over the city to draw near, even every man with his destroying weapon in his hand. And, behold, six men came from the way of the higher gate [men of authority], *which lieth toward the north, and every man a slaughter weapon in his hand; and one man among them was clothed with linen, with a writer's inkhorn by his side* [he represents the baptized saints before the destruction of Jerusalem, with the Holy Spirit in them, going around baptizing people with blood and fire]....*And he called to the man clothed with linen, which had the writer's inkhorn by his side; and the LORD said unto him, Go through the midst of the city, through the midst of Jerusalem, and set a mark upon the foreheads of the men that sigh and that cry for all the abominations that be done in the midst thereof.*

The Holy Spirit

And to the others [the destroying army] *he said in mine hearing, Go ye after him through the city, and smite: let not your eye spare, neither have ye pity: slay utterly old and young, both maids, and little children, and women: but come not near any man upon whom is the mark; and begin at my sanctuary. Then they began at the ancient men which were before the house. And he said unto them, Defile the house, and fill the courts with the slain: go ye forth. And they went forth, and slew in the city. And it came to pass, while they were slaying them, and I was left, that I fell upon my face, and cried, and said, Ah Lord GOD! wilt thou destroy all the residue of Israel in thy pouring out of thy fury upon Jerusalem? Then said he unto me, The iniquity of the house of Israel and Judah is exceeding great, and the land is full of blood, and the city full of perverseness: for they say, The LORD hath forsaken the earth.* (Ezek. 9:1–9)

That is what they say today, that the Lord does not see anymore. *"As for me also* [He caused me to know that He lives]*, mine eye shall not spare, neither will I have pity, but I will recompense their way upon their head"* (v. 10).

"And, behold, the man clothed with linen, which had the inkhorn by his side, reported the matter, saying, I have done as thou hast commanded me" (v. 11). It is done; I have finished. The last one is sealed, and the door is closed.

Ezekiel had this vision nearly six hundred years before Jesus came, prior to the destruction of Jerusalem, and now it has been about twenty-six hundred years since he saw that vision—the vision of Jerusalem, of the church, and of the conditions of the world, especially of the church. Today, we are living in a time in the world and the church that is parallel to the time of the destruction of Jerusalem. The same remarkable things are taking place today—just before the Great Tribulation, just before the wrath of God is poured out without mercy on the people. The Lord showed the prophet the awful condition of His people, and these things came upon the Jewish nation. But this time they will come upon the whole world.

The Jewish nation had sinned against God. They were God's special people—God's called-out people. He said, "I did not call you out because you were the greatest people, the strongest people, the wealthiest people, the best people, for you were the fewest of all. Yet I have called you, chosen you, set My love upon you." (See Deuteronomy 7:6–8.) God's chosen people have always been few.

To the Jewish people came the Law and the Prophets, and then Christ. God gave the Law from Mount Sinai amid mighty signs and wonders. When the temple was dedicated, the presence of God was seen. Over the years, God appeared to His people. He gave them priests and prophets, revelations from heaven, spiritual signs, and visions. Angels appeared. God talked from heaven and did all these things while His people obeyed. But soon they got proud, haughty, and lifted up. They began to glory in their multiplying numbers; they began to take in people from other nations whose hearts were not right with God and to give them power and high places of authority and great advantage. These people were given charge over God's holy people, and they ruled them with a rod of iron.

God's people began to follow the wisdom of men. He warned them and warned them and finally began to show them that they had left the Fountainhead of living waters and had hewed out broken cisterns that could not hold water (Jer. 2:13).

The Holy Spirit

The glory of God appeared to Ezekiel, picked him up by the hair on his head, carried him through space between heaven and earth, and set him down in Jerusalem. God told him to look and see the dreadful things. The holy places were filled with pictures of serpents, like Devil worship today, things that were unclean. God showed him all the abominations. He took him into the holiest place where twenty-five men sat with their backs to God and worshipped the sun. (See Ezekiel 8:1–16.)

Then God told Ezekiel, "Now you go and take the example of the temple in all its glory, when the glory of God filled the house (Ezek. 10:4), and you warn these people. Take the example of the glorious temple, and go and compare it with the example today. Show them where they have failed, and see if they will repent." God said they would never do it (Ezek. 3:7). But God does not say we are to run things to suit ourselves. They were warned.

"Son of man, I am not sending you to the heathen, but to the people of the house of Israel." (See Ezekiel 3:4–6.) But they would not hear. They failed to know that the prophet of God was in their midst. He stood and warned them, but it did not do any good.

Pretty soon, the last prophet came to Israel, and they rejected him. Then the love and mercy and glory of God left them. For nearly four hundred years, perhaps longer, the children of Israel were left without holy priests, without prophets, and without visions or revelations—except for a few humble believers, brokenhearted little ones, who were true to God.

The people began to say, "Oh, God, how long? There is no one who can speak to us anymore. We have no prophets, priests, visions, or revelations. Where are the signs?" All through the Word of God, when people were right with Him, they saw signs of the invisible God. But when they backslid, they lost the connection. The pipe got filled up, and the flow of living water stopped. They trusted in broken cisterns (Jer. 2:13)—man's wealth and knowledge, which is an abomination without God.

The Signs of the Times

That is the condition the Jews were in when Christ came. Yet after they had been looking for Him for nearly four hundred years, they did not know Him. He said to them, "Why is it that you do not discern the signs of the time? Your prophecies are fulfilled, and you are living in the days when the Son of Man has come." (See Luke 12:56.) But they were saying, "God has forsaken the earth. God doesn't see. God has left the earth, and the signs and wonders are all gone." (See Ezekiel 8:12; 9:9.) They began to follow men's wisdom. They did not want the power of God. They left the *"fountain of living waters"* (Jer. 2:13). They did not want to hear a shout in the camp (see 1 Samuel 4:5); they did not want to see God's power. And so it is now.

But God is love. God does hear, and He helps you to see that. God will visit the earth again.

When Jesus came, He gave the people another call just like the *"latter rain"* (Joel 2:23). Yet the apostle Paul said that the Day of the Lord would not come without a *"falling away"* (2 Thess. 2:3). God knows how they fell away. Before Jesus came, His coming was prophesied, and when He came, the Jewish nation had another chance—He offered them the kingdom. But they spurned Him and turned Him away, and finally one day He wept over them bitterly, saying, "O Jerusalem, how often would I have gathered you from the destruction that is coming. Now I leave you." (See Matthew 23:37–39; Luke 19:41–44.) And that is just what He is saying today. "This time your house is left unto you desolate (Matt. 23:38). Your city will be destroyed. The enemy is coming; armies are coming in to lay your place desolate (Luke 19:43), and the blood will flow like rivers."

But remember that God warned His faithful people about the destruction of Jerusalem that occurred in A.D. 70. He had a people who had accepted Christ, and they had followed the Lamb. They waited in Jerusalem until they were baptized with the Holy Spirit, and God revealed Himself and His Word to them. Christ had told his disciples one day, when speaking of the temple, "The day is coming when that beautiful temple will be destroyed. Not one stone will be left upon another, and the city will be destroyed." (See Matthew 24:1–2; Luke 19:43–44.) The disciples said, "Lord, tell us when that evil thing will happen. We want to know what will be the sign of Your second coming and of the end of the world" (Matt. 24:3). Jesus told them and gave them signs so that we can know them today.

Jesus is coming soon; the signs show He will come back soon. We are concerned about the signs. The disciples asked questions; they were serious about asking, and the Lord told them how they would know. He gave them signs and said, "When you see certain signs come to pass, prepare to flee to the mountains; make ready to escape. Then there will be other signs and finally a certain sign. When you see this sign, if you have not made all your preparations for flight, if you are on the housetop, do not go back into the house. If you are in the field, do not turn back to take your coat, but flee to the mountains. Get out of the city, because the gates will be closed, and you will be shut in." (See Matthew 24:3–18.)

The disciples believed what God said. They took His Word by faith; they believed the Word and felt the responsibility. They loved their people, and they knew that unless their people accepted Jesus Christ, they would not escape. They were in the right; they were baptized saints sighing and crying (see Ezekiel 9:4) for their families and for their neighbors, sighing and crying on account of the dreadful things going on. However, they were shut in with God. They had the mark of God upon them.

When you see the things that are making the world turn pale and tremble—when these things come to pass—lift up your heads and rejoice. Rejoice at every calamity, because it will soon be over. Although the disciples sighed and cried, they still rejoiced because they knew they were saved.

The man with the inkhorn represents the people of the Holy Spirit. In a short time, all these things are coming. Get busy and warn the people. *"Whether they hear or whether they refuse"* (Ezek. 2:5 NKJV), warn the people.

Imagine the early believers who were filled with the Holy Spirit. Imagine them going through offices and stores and business places in Jerusalem, doing their best to warn the people. The soldiers who were coming in that great army of destruction were going back and forth about their business. The man with the inkhorn was to do the work, to get ready for the great work, but no one in Jerusalem knew what was going on. The saints of God were going everywhere, warning the people the best they could.

The believers told them, "Judgment is coming; destruction is coming; the city will be taken." The disciples were laughed at as fools, fanatics, and enemies. The people would not listen to them. But the saints knew that when the destruction came, the city would be taken, and the people's businesses would be no good. The enemy would take everything; their houses and lands would amount to nothing. The only thing they could do was to use their money to warn the people that destruction was coming. So their money, their gold, their silver, and their land would not do any good. Neither will yours do you any good. May God help you to see this truth and to use your time and resources to spread the Gospel.

God's Mark on the Forehead

"Blow the trumpet in Zion" (Joel 2:15)! Jerusalem will be taken; tribulation is coming. The Day of the Lord is near; it hurries greatly. It is even at the door (Matt. 24:33). Warn the people that they must have the seal of God on their foreheads (Ezek. 9:4; see also Revelation 7:3). That is why we are going around getting the people saved, baptized with the Holy Spirit, and sealed with the finger of the living God. They have to have the mark of God on their foreheads to understand these things. Go through the streets of the city; note those who sigh and cry, and seal them with the finger of God (Ezek. 9:4). That is what God is doing today. Glory to God.

The Blood and Fire Mark

That is what they did at the time of the destruction of Jerusalem. The Word went out. The believers were laughed at and scorned and persecuted, but they saw the signs coming faster. The more they did, the more the people laughed at them and persecuted them. They hid away in the mountains, and every day they felt worse about their friends and neighbors; they would hasten into the city and try to show the people that these things were true. The people did not believe, but that did not change the fact.

It was at the time of the great Feast of Passover that Jesus told His disciples what would be the signs of the destruction. Rabbis and many people from all over the world were there. While they were gathered there, the Lord told them, "When you see a certain signal, get out quickly. Don't go back to take anything out of your house, but get out of the city." (See Matthew 24:15–17.)

However, when the time came, they would not believe anything; they were having a good time. But at last a certain signal came, and the gates were closed; they were shut in, and they never got out. But those who had the seal of the living God upon them were "caught up"—taken out—just like we will be when the time comes. Josephus, the historian, tells us that not one of the followers of Jesus Christ went down in the slaughter. They believed God and prepared for the escape, and God took every baptized saint. Not one was permitted to be locked up in that city because they believed God and made preparations for flight. Hallelujah.

Today, the people of God are a nation that is hated, a *"nation not desired"* (Zeph. 2:1), a nation despised. This "sect" is spoken against everywhere (Acts 28:22), and I am glad I am one of them. When Jesus comes, you will be willing to be called a fanatic, a Holy Roller, or anything else. May God help you to see it.

The people of Jerusalem were all taken unawares. The enemy came, the gates were shut, and the greatest calamity that the world ever saw fell upon the Jews. When the army went into the city, they went into the inner court where the holy men—twenty-five of them—sat with their backs to God. (See Ezekiel 8:16.) They commenced with these fat priests and heads of the church, and they were slaughtered like oxen. We are told that the people in the city had no provisions; they were shut in there and literally starved to death. Delicate women ate their own children. Delicate women who would not put their feet on the ground ate their own children during that siege. Such a thing had never happened before. You know all about these things. Some were carried away in captivity, and only a few despised little ones were left as slaves. But God had revealed the knowledge of this destruction to His people who had the mark, and every last one escaped. Oh, hallelujah!

The prophet Ezekiel is looking down in history to us today, warning us in just the same way. When Jesus comes, there will be tribulation and a time of trouble on the earth such as was never known before. The darkness will be so great that people will be able to feel it. When Jesus comes to catch His bride away, there will be a time such as the world never heard of before. All who sigh and cry for the abominable things that are going on in the world, those who have the mark, are children of the day (Ezek. 9:4). You will not be overtaken as by a *"thief in the night"* (1 Thess. 5:2), for you are the children of light. The wise will know. Glory to God.

The Blood and Fire Mark

History tells us that many rich men and many great men went down in the siege; but those who were called, who had God's mark, who were wanderers and pilgrims and had to leave their homes and wealth, escaped with their lives and a few little things that they could take away to provide for their comfort. When Jesus returns for His bride, you won't take anything. All will be left for the Devil to work with, for the world will go on just like it is now. When Jesus comes, it will not yet be the end of the world. But the bride, the saints, will be taken up.

Dear friends, we are living in a day parallel to the time of the destruction of Jerusalem. Jesus is coming again. In preparation, God is visiting the earth again, pouring out His Spirit.

The church has gone back to a state of weakness. When I was a girl, the Methodist church was the most powerful and the most spiritual. People fell under the power of God, danced, and did lots of other things. They had an "amen corner" in every church. When the preacher came in, he would not stop for anything, but would go into the pulpit, open the Bible, and begin. He would not say, "My second point is..." and "My third point is..." for he did not have time. The amens came from all over the house. The people obeyed God; they were happy people, and they had great power.

But today people are saying, "We don't know God. He has left us. We don't see Him. We don't like these fanatical meetings." So today there is not an amen or a shout from anybody. If one sister gets blessed, and the power of God comes on her, and she shouts, three or four good sisters get around her, and she never shouts again.

The Holy Spirit

Lots of people are wrong today if those good old people were right. Dear friends, if they were right, then your own fathers, mothers, and grandparents—and you yourself—would not like to have anyone say they were crazy. If they were right before God, someone is wrong today.

Now, listen, God is pouring out His Spirit again on all nations of the earth. Today God has a baptized people. Saints of every nation, tribe, and church are mixed up in this company who are baptized in the Holy Spirit and fire and who are risking everything to warn the people. They are working to get people saved and baptized with the Holy Spirit. Get under the blood, and get the mark of the living God on your forehead. God is visiting you again, and we are just on the eve of the awful tribulations.

War, Famine, and Pestilence

Men and women will eat their own children. There will be war, famine, and pestilence, and all these things in one day. God says that it will be that way. Devilish appetite is going to get into animals of all kinds, into the wild beasts. This problem will be compounded because famine is coming and the animals will leave the wilderness and come into the cities to get something to eat. (See Ezekiel 5:17.) If you escape the war, the wild beasts will get you. If you escape the lions and bears and stagger around in your own house for a quiet place to die, a serpent will bite you. (See Amos 5:19.)

Don't you see that these things are coming? God has not left you without warning. Read the Word of God and watch the signs; watch the signs and read the Word. These things were seen twenty-six hundred years ago. A day with the Lord is only a little while, and a thousand years is like only a day to Him (2 Pet. 3:8).

We are the people on the stage of action today, and the people living today will be in this great army of slaughter. But the saints will be taken out. They will never see death but will see the Son of God coming in glory.

So, every day, everywhere, we see the signs being fulfilled that Jesus is coming. One great sign is that God's real saints are making such an effort to go throughout the world with the Gospel. They are risking everything to enlighten the people, to find hearts who will receive the message, get saved, and let God seal them with the seal of the living God on their foreheads. Let us make the vision plain. May God help me to do so. Will the people see that we are actors in this vision? Let us make it plain so that those who hear may understand and, when they receive the seal of God, will run to get ready. That is what we are doing today.

Now, beloved, we must have this mark of God. We must not only be saved but sealed with the seal of the living God. It may be that if you go deep enough, you will be hidden away from all these things that are coming on the earth. Be shut in with God today—now.

The angels represented as holding back the four winds of the earth (Rev. 7:1) are letting loose now, as surely as God lives. Another great angel is crying, "Hold on a little longer." We wonder about these things. Angels see the awful condition of the earth: the cup of iniquity is full. They ask, "O Lord, can we let loose? Can the sun be turned on to scorch men? Can the cyclones tear down the cedars? Can the tidal waves sweep the towns away? Can the earthquakes come?" But the great angel who carries the Gospel of Jesus Christ says, "Hold on a little longer; hold on a little longer. Don't let loose. Hold back the power of the sun; hold back the greatest tidal waves, the greatest cyclones, the greatest earthquakes, and the greatest calamities, until we have sealed the servants of God with the seal of the living God on their foreheads."

You may be a servant of God, but you must be sealed with the seal of God; you must have the mark of blood and fire; you must be sealed with the seal of the living God. Jesus is saying, "Hold back the great calamities; they would be a great inconvenience to My servants. They are the lights of the world (Matt. 5:14). For the sake of the souls who want to be saved, I will give my people a little more chance to work. Don't let loose."

Hold back! What for? Hold back until we have sealed the saints of God with the seal of the living God on the forehead. My God, help these people to see why the sun does not get two or three degrees hotter and kill millions. Don't you see the signs of what is coming? One hundred died in the heat in Chicago. If the sun had been a few more degrees hotter, millions would have died.

Watch and pray. Be in an attitude of prayer or praise all the time so that you may be counted worthy to escape these awful calamities and stand before the Son of God (Luke 21:36). Don't you see that we have no time for foolish talking about what this one or that one said? I am here to tell what Jesus Christ said. I don't steal words from my neighbor. It is what Jesus said that is important. We are to pay attention to *"Thus saith the Lord."* (See, for example, Ezekiel 2:4.)

The Blood and Fire Mark

In that day, two will be sleeping in the same bed; one will be taken and the other left. Two will be working in the field; one will talk and talk all kinds of foolishness, and the other will be obliged to answer; then suddenly there will be no answer. The first one will look up and say, "Why, what is the matter, my friend? Where did you go?" He is alone; his friend is gone. Find him if you can. He escaped before the gates were shut. Glory to God, he was caught away. (See Matthew 24:37–42.)

That is going to be just the way it is when Jesus comes. He will take His saints up alive; they will be changed quicker than a wink. We will not have other bodies, but our bodies will be very light. We are not waiting for wings; rather, we are looking for the power from heaven to lighten these bodies. We will rise like He did. Our hands and feet will be like wings. We will go sailing through the air—up over the stars—to meet the Lord with a shout. (See 1 Thessalonians 4:16–17.) Glory to God!

A Fountain of Tears

But for those who are left, it will be so different. Those who reject Christ will be left to go down. Oh, God, how we ought to be sighing and crying for the people who will be left. We don't sigh enough; we don't cry enough. But at the same time, we are so full of joy that we have to release it or explode. Be glad that you are living in the time of the *"latter rain"* (Joel 2:23). Rejoice and be glad.

Along with our joy, we are sighing and crying because of the corruption. Several times I have cried out—the Holy Spirit within me has cried out. It came to me like the prophet said when he was speaking of this day: *"My bowels, my bowels!"* (Jer. 4:19). His body seemed to be bursting, and his head was a fountain of tears, because of the destruction that is coming on the earth. Jesus is weeping over Jerusalem, and how the Holy Spirit weeps through me! It seems as though I will cry until I die. But I try to go on.

God is putting a mark on those who sigh and cry for all the abominable things that are coming on the earth. Dear friends, don't you see that the angels want to let loose the four winds? They are saying, "Oh, can we let loose? The people are so wicked; let the people go." No, not until we have sealed the servants of God with the seal of the living God on their foreheads. Go through the streets, and put a mark upon everyone who sighs and cries. Put the mark of God on them. Tell them to be baptized in the Holy Spirit. Jesus Christ will baptize you with the Holy Spirit and fire (Matt. 3:11). He will give us wisdom—the mind of Christ. He will seal us with knowledge, and we will not be left in the dark but will be children of light.

You say that you are saved and living pure, holy lives before God; however, if you don't get this baptism and get the everlasting arms of Jesus around you, you will be carried away in the throng, and you will not be ready to go up when Jesus comes. Oh, hold back until the servants of God get the light and are sealed with the seal of the living God on their foreheads.

There is not much time. The Lord is holding back these things. Are we about our Master's business? No wonder I don't rest—I am trusting God to carry me through. I know these things are true. God help us, the world is getting pretty well shut in now. There are so many false doctrines of the Devil coming in. People are believing in delusions. You must keep under the blood, or you will be carried away. I praise God for the knowledge that Jesus is coming soon. Praise His name forever.

These awful things are already on the earth. You know the Lord said that when certain things happen, it is the *"beginning of sorrows"* (Matt. 24:8). The nations are mad. Aren't they mad now? They are crazy. What are they fighting for? Jealous hatred. One nation is against another; several have gone down. Look at them. No one knows the real truth. May God help you to hear. This is the beginning of sorrows. The four winds are going to be let loose, as surely as you live. If this is the beginning of sorrows, what will the end be?

You may escape the worst things and be hidden away. The prophet, looking down to the last days, saw the saints going up. He says, "Come up, my people, and enter into the place prepared for you. Shut the doors after you, and hide for a little while, for the Lord is coming down to punish the inhabitants of the earth. Their blood will flow like the dust, and their flesh will lie like the dung (Zeph. 1:17); they will not be buried." In the World War, tens of thousands have been burned, and nobody knows where they are. Isn't that being fulfilled now? If this is only the beginning of sorrows, what will the end be? God is holding back the worst things. Europe has had the call. They have been warned and warned.

God gave a wonderful vision to a man who was raised to be a Catholic priest. Two angels visited him in the night and caused him to stand before a great congregation and warn the people of these awful calamities. He told two thousand people that Europe had been warned but that the people of Europe had turned their backs and rejected God, and now He is warning them at the mouth of the cannon.

The United States is the same way. God is giving the people here the last call—the last chance to be sealed with the seal of the living God, but they turn Him away. The last one will soon be sealed. God will call at the mouth of the cannon. This country will be bathed in blood after a while. The best thing is to hide away. May God help us to be up and doing, to be clothed in white linen, which is the righteousness of the saints, with the writer's inkhorn, which is the Holy Spirit working through us, calling the people to get right with God. Ask God for knowledge and wisdom; get the resurrection power in your body; and, when Jesus comes, be snatched out of this world.

"We who are alive and remain until the coming of the Lord will by no means precede those who are asleep" (1 Thess. 4:15 NKJV). The dead in Christ will rise first and shake off the dust and worms like dew and will go up with a shout. Praise the Lord! They will be ahead of us. Don't worry about the dead who died in Christ; when Jesus comes, God will bring them with Him. In honor of His Son's wedding, God is getting to meet the bride. The dead saints will be caught up first, and they will come with God the Father when Christ comes to catch His bride away. We do not need to worry about the dead who are in Christ. They will come up. But the time is near.

It will not be very long until we who are alive will meet them in the air. I will meet my husband who has died. He said, "I am not looking to the grave at all." But his body is there, and different saints in visions have seen him go up in his glorified body; he will be one of the first to meet me when I rise in the air. Many dear saints have died shouting and have gone to glory. They will be raised, and I will meet them. All our dear friends who have died in Christ will be raised first. We will rise in our glorified, immortal bodies to meet the Lord in the air.

Now, beloved, don't let this message run off you. Let it burn in your hearts, because it is a message from the Lord. Hallelujah. It may be something you have never heard before, but you are hearing it now. You see the parallel with the time of the prophet Ezekiel; you see the danger. Don't you see it? Oh, believe it: you are being warned. Take your Bibles; ask God about us whom you think are so foolish. Oh, glory to God; I am glad I am foolish enough to believe God. I am glad I am getting light enough to go up in the air when He comes. Hallelujah! Glory! Some of the resurrection power! Praise the Lord! I am looking forward to going up in the sky—up in the air—not to the grave. Glory to God. Hallelujah!

Chapter 14

The Seal of God on His People

Gather yourselves together, yea, gather together, O nation not desired; before the decree bring forth, before the day pass as the chaff, before the fierce anger of the LORD come upon you, before the day of the LORD's anger come upon you. Seek ye the LORD, all ye meek of the earth, which have wrought his judgment; seek righteousness, seek meekness: it may be ye shall be hid in the day of the LORD's anger.
—Zephaniah 2:1–3

This call is not to sinners, but to God's servants, to His children, to eat the *"strong meat"* (Heb. 5:14): *"Ye meek of the earth, which have wrought His judgment."*

You understand that you are saved, and you are working somewhat for the Lord, but He calls you to seek Him in a different way and for a different meekness. In this passage, He cries to you three times: to seek the Lord, to seek righteousness, and to seek meekness.

He is giving you the call to the Marriage Supper, calling you to get oil in your vessels (see Matthew 25:1–13), to get baptized with the Holy Spirit, to be sealed on the forehead with the seal of the living God, which is the seal of promise.

The Holy Spirit will also bear witness through you in other tongues, for you may have any of the gifts. You will have power as a witness after the Holy Spirit has come upon you (Acts 1:8).

The prophet Zephaniah warns you to escape the awful judgments that are now coming on the earth. It may be that you will be hidden in the Day of the Lord's anger. This is the only hope for you to escape the awful destruction that is about to sweep over the world, for there is no other hiding place, no other safety in the world. Oh, that you may be hidden in the Day of His wrath!

Yes, you may be, but whether or not you will be hidden in that Day depends on how far and how deep you get hidden away in God's love and power and will. You may be hidden. He shows that His judgments will burst on the earth like a whirlwind and that the wicked will be like chaff.

Dear reader, there is no doubt, according to God's Word and the signs all around us and the revelations and warnings the Lord is now giving us through His Spirit, that this is the time and we are the people. We have no time to lose, for *"behold, he cometh"* (Rev. 1:7) and is even now at the door (Matt. 24:33).

The text implies haste: Awake. Arise. Rouse yourselves. Flee to Christ. Get oil in your vessels. Shout the cry, *"Behold, the bridegroom cometh!"* (Matt. 25:6). Trim your lamps. Get sealed with wisdom so that you may be among the wise who will sit with Christ on His throne to judge the nations. Gather yourselves together. Yes, gather together.

"O nation not desired." No one wants this people who have come out of darkness into this marvelous light (1 Pet. 2:9), this *"peculiar people"* (v. 9), who appear foolish on account of the supernatural power and visible works of the Spirit.

We are hated and despised and forsaken. Our name is cast out as evil; we are misrepresented and counted as the outcasts of the earth, but we are very much beloved in heaven.

When the prophet Daniel was asking God to explain these signs that we now see, Jesus appeared to him and sent the angel to him to make the vision clear. The angel said, *"O Daniel, a man greatly beloved, understand the* [vision and the] *words"* (Dan. 10:11). Then again, *"O man greatly beloved, fear not: peace be unto thee"* (v. 19).

The Sound of the Bugle Call

We are the people that the Lord was showing Daniel. Now the same loving words of cheer come to us through His Spirit, to the *"little flock"* (Luke 12:32), the bride that is making herself ready (Rev. 19:7): *"'To him that overcometh will I grant to sit with me in my throne'* (Rev. 3:21). Fear not, for I am with you; you are much beloved."

The Lord is sounding the bugle call through some believers in a most remarkable way by the Holy Spirit. It almost sounds as if the Judgment Day is here. It makes the people tremble. He is calling His saints together so that we will see eye to eye when He brings us to the heavenly Zion. *"Blow ye the trumpet in Zion, and sound an alarm in my holy mountain'* (Joel 2:1), among the saints. Let all the people tremble. Go gather My saints together, who have made a covenant with Me by sacrifice."

May God help us to make the right kind of sacrifice. Oh, praise the Lord, that is my calling today, to get the saints together in one spirit, one faith, and one mind (Phil. 1:27), filled with love and oneness in Christ, lost and swallowed up in Him and in His love and power.

In the chapter preceding our Scripture text, the Lord shows us the awful trials and the time of the Great Tribulation:

> *The great day of the Lord is near, it is near, and hasteth greatly, even the voice of the day of the Lord: the mighty man shall cry there bitterly. That day is a day of wrath, a day of trouble and distress, a day of wasteness and desolation, a day of darkness and gloominess, a day of clouds and thick darkness, a day of the trumpet and alarm against the fenced cities, and against the high towers. And I will bring distress upon men, that they shall walk like blind men, because they have sinned against the Lord: and their blood shall be poured out as dust, and their flesh as the dung. Neither their silver nor their gold shall be able to deliver them in the day of the Lord's wrath; but the whole land shall be devoured by the fire of his jealousy: for he shall make even a speedy riddance of all them that dwell in the land.* (Zeph. 1:14–18)

He has given us this fearful warning; therefore, gather yourselves together. Oh, gather together, so that you may be hidden in the day of His wrath.

The Seal of God on His People

We are a nation among the nations:

But ye are a chosen generation, a royal priesthood, an holy nation, a peculiar people; that ye should show forth the praises of him who hath called you out of darkness into his marvellous light. (1 Pet. 2:9)

We are called out in this generation. We are a holy nation, a nation of kings and priests, called out from among men. We are royal because we are children of the King, a holy priesthood, heirs to a throne.

Unto him that loved us, and washed us from our sins in his own blood, and hath made us kings and priests unto God and his Father; to him be glory and dominion for ever and ever. Amen. (Rev. 1:5–6)

Thou wast slain, and hast redeemed us to God by thy blood out of every kindred, and tongue, and people, and nation; and hast made us unto our God kings and priests: and we shall reign on the earth. (Rev. 5:9–10)

This is the kind of praise that will go on in heaven after Jesus has taken His bride there. Shouting these praises will be the believers who were counted worthy to be hidden away in the City of Gold, the place prepared for them, which Jesus had promised (John 14:2–3). The great Marriage will have taken place. The long-waiting bride will have been made the Lamb's wife. They will all be enjoying the great Marriage Supper of the Lamb. They will be receiving their crowns and positions in glory. They will be taking their thrones and exalted stations, which their diplomas call for and which they had gained down here in the Holy Spirit school.

The Holy Spirit

Hear the shouting; they make the heavens ring, amid all the brightness and glory of heaven. Oh, how wonderful is the meeting of the loved ones who will never part! They are safe, home safe at last.

Jesus is the attraction. He is the One. All eyes are on Him; all are trying to get nearest Him and to give Him all honor and glory, for through His blood and power they have entered into His glory.

Yes, the saints were safe in heaven while the dreadful work of destruction was going on in the earth. They knew they were coming back to earth to rule with kingly authority, to bless the people with priestly power. God has made them kings and priests unto Him, and they will reign on the earth a thousand years (Rev. 5:10; 20:6). *"The saints shall judge the world"* (1 Cor. 6:2). They are rejoicing because they are coming back to earth.

Chapter 15

Some Will Not Taste Death

Verily I say unto you, There be some standing here,
which shall not taste of death, till they see the Son
of man coming in his kingdom. And after six days
Jesus taketh Peter, James, and John his brother, and
bringeth them up into an high mountain apart, and
was transfigured before them: and his face did shine
as the sun, and his raiment was white as the light.
—Matthew 16:28–17:2

H e was the Son of Man, and He was the Son of God. He *"shall come in the glory of his Father with his angels; and then he shall reward every man according to his works"* (Matt. 16:27), according to the deeds done while in the body.

Jesus said, *"Verily I say unto you, there be some standing here, which shall not taste of death, till they see the Son of man coming in his kingdom."* Six days later—literal days—Jesus took Peter, James, and James's brother John, and brought them up into a high mountain by themselves, and He was transfigured before them. His face shone as the sun, and His clothing was as white as the light.

> *And, behold, there appeared unto them Moses and Elias talking with him. Then answered Peter, and said unto Jesus, Lord, it is good for us to be here: if thou wilt, let us make here three tabernacles; one for thee, and one for Moses, and one for Elias.*
> (Matt. 17:3–4)

Peter did not know what he was talking about. But God settled the question:

> *While he yet spake, behold, a bright cloud overshadowed them: and behold a voice out of the cloud, which said, This is my beloved Son, in whom I am well pleased; hear ye him.*
> (v. 5)

Glory to God! Hallelujah! Glory to Jesus!

There is a great deal in this lesson. It shows the kingdom of Christ that is very close at hand now, and the translation of the saints. It shows the Tribulation that is coming on the earth. It shows the close of the Tribulation when Christ will come back with His saints, bind the Devil, destroy the Antichrist and his army, and set up the glorious Millennium.

Jesus had earlier said to His disciples, *"There be some standing here, which shall not taste of death, till they see the Son of man coming in his kingdom."* These were six natural, literal days, for just six days afterward, the disciples saw on the Mount of Transfiguration what Jesus said they would see. However, these six days also apply to us. In prophetic terms, a day equals a year, and a day with the Lord is as a thousand years. (See 2 Peter 3:8.) There were four "days" before Christ came—four thousand years. The last two "days" bring us down to today, and make six thousand years. So we are on the stage of action today; we are right at the close of the last day. On the sixth day, close to the seventh day, we will be ushered into the great Millennium, the thousand years of rest, the Sabbath Day.

Jesus speaks to us with as much force today, and He applies this to us, as He did to them.

A Display of Heavenly Glory

"Some of you who are standing here will never experience death until you see My coming kingdom, for I will come in all the glory of My Father's kingdom, with all the holy angels, and I will come in My own kingly glory. I will give you a display of this glory; you will never experience death until you see this thing."

The disciples did not understand; but six days afterward, it came to pass. Jesus took Peter, James, and John—those who always seemed to be nearest the Master, more anxious to stand by Him than the rest—and they were initiated into a good many things the rest did not know. He took these three, slipped away from the rest, and brought them up into the mountain. That was six natural days from when He said, *There be some standing here, which shall not taste of death, till they see the Son of man coming in his kingdom.*

Hallelujah to Jesus! Let us think about how this applies to us. The prophecies are fulfilled, and Christ's return will be just a very short time now, according to

God's Word. I say to you today, this applies to us. "I am coming in My kingdom in all the glory of the eternal world to catch my bride away. Some of you will never experience death until you see this and take part in it." Glory to God! Hallelujah!

God Turns to His People Again

The prophecies point to this time. This is the end of the Gentile age (see Luke 21:24)—the Gentile age is to wind up at the close of the sixth day. The Jews are saying, "Come, let us return to the Lord, for we have been wounded and bruised, and He will heal us. The second day He will revive us, and early in the morning of the third day, He will raise us up. (See Hosea 6:1–2.)

This is the second day. The Jews are being wonderfully revived all over the land; they never had such renown. They are reviving; their chains are being broken. But early in the morning—it will only be a few days, bless God—He will raise us up. He will also raise them up from the grave, and wonderful things are going to take place. Before the Great Tribulation, the saints will be taken up. Jesus Christ will stand up for His people, and there will be a time of trouble on the earth such as the world has never known, and never will know again, when the dead in Christ will rise and the saints will be taken up.

So we are coming into the time when these prophecies are coming on the earth. These are the *"beginning of sorrows"* (Matt. 24:8), and if this is only the beginning, what will the end be? This is the preparation time when He will disseminate the power of the holy people all over the world as a witness. God will rise up in

His power and majesty, and God will work His *"strange work"* (Isa. 28:21) by the Holy Spirit through His saints. Natural men do not understand this.

Jesus is coming in His kingdom. Get out of the city of destruction. Run up on the mountain. Bless God. Be ready for the *"manifestation of the sons of God"* (Rom. 8:19). This is the preparation time. This is the last message. Jesus said, "This Gospel of My kingdom will be preached in the last days of My preparation as a witness to all the world—to every nation. Then the end will come." (See Matthew 24:14.)

Christ will come and take a prepared people out for Himself—a people to be His bride—and then the awful darkness will cover the earth. The Tribulation time will set in; the time of trouble will continue until the Battle of Armageddon, when the Antichrist will be destroyed and two-thirds of all the earth will go down in war, famine, and pestilences (Matt. 24:7) and be devoured by wild beasts. But one-third will withstand the Antichrist and escape all the troubles and calamities that will come on this earth. (See Zechariah 13:8.) They will go through the fire, persecution, and famine, and when Jesus comes back to bind the Devil and cast him into the pit, one-third of the earth will run out to meet Him and acknowledge Him as their Lord of Lords. He will forgive their sins and call them His people; they will call Him their God (v. 9), and they will be restored at Jerusalem.

God has said it. He said that He will take His bride away; then, at the end of the Tribulation, He will return with His bride, riding on the white horse of power (Rev. 19:11–16). He will come back to build up the *"waste places of Jerusalem"* (Isa. 52:9) so that the remnant of men might seek the Lord. All the Gentiles who have called on His name will be in that company of the one-third who won't go down in the tribulations. He is coming back with the saints at the end of the Tribulation to destroy the Antichrist, and the blood will come up to the horses' bridles (Rev. 14:20).

The prophet John saw a great angel standing in the sun and calling with a loud voice to the fowls of the air, "Come gather yourselves together for the great supper of the great God, so that you may eat the flesh of the kings and of the mighty men of the earth, and those who sat upon horses, and the flesh of the horses, and so that you may drink their blood." (See Revelation 19:17–18.)

The Antichrist and his army will be destroyed when God calls the wild beasts and the fowls of the air to eat their carcasses, at the time when Jesus comes back and binds the Devil and casts him into the pit for one thousand years (Rev. 20:2–3). But the one-third who have gone through everything and escaped by the hand of God will come out to meet the Lord with gladness. He will accept them and forgive them, and He will call them His people. They will be established, and the glorious Millennium will be ushered in. But before this, the saints of God will be caught up to Christ (1 Thess. 4:17). He is coming to take His people out of the world, and everyone who is not ready to go up will be left behind and will go down when the Antichrist comes forth.

The time of the awful Tribulation is near. May the Lord help us to understand this, dear friends. The enemies of the Lord today are getting worse and worse. The cup of iniquity is full; the harvest of the earth is ripe and ready to be cut down and cast into the winepress of the wrath of God Almighty. So God is pouring out His Spirit. Glory hallelujah! He is bringing about signs and wonders through His holy vessels, which will scatter the power of God through the land. And the great angels are saying, "May we not loose the four winds?" (See Revelation 7:1.)

When will all these wonders—these unusual works of God coming up in the preparation time—cease? Not that they are wonders in themselves; they are wonders because they are part of God's time of preparation. There is no end to these unusual works of God.

God's Day of Preparation

The Lord says, "I will rise up and work my strange works in the day of preparation." Therefore, do not be mockers. Behold, I have the message from the Lord; the decree has gone forth, and He will make a speedy riddance of all the mockers on the face of the earth. They don't laugh at a cyclone; they don't laugh at a great fire; but they will laugh and mock at God's *"strange work"* (Isa. 28:21). Do not be mockers, for I have received the message from the Lord. It came from heaven, and the decree has already gone forth. God will make a speedy riddance of all the mockers on the face of the earth. (See verses 21–22.)

This is God's work. He is giving the people a warning. He is pouring out His Spirit upon the earth for the last time, in order to warn the people just before the *"notable day of the Lord come*[s]" (Acts 2:20). Repent and turn to the Lord, and you will be saved. Every nation will be warned through the mighty display of God's power. God's mighty works are the visible signs that He is here, the visible manifestations that this is God's message—the last message—and that God, through His people, is pouring out the Holy Spirit.

We do not have a dead God or a dead Christ. He lives forever, and He is here right now. God is dispersing power over the land and warning the people against the things that are coming. Everyone who has the mark of fire and blood will be caught up to heaven. Every last one. And then the Antichrist will come forth—the awful Antichrist, the Man of Sin. He will come forth in his awful power after the Hinderer, the One who restrains the lawlessness, is taken away. (See 2 Thessalonians 2:7 NKJV.)

Who is the Hinderer? The Holy Spirit, working through the body of Christ. *"Ye are the light of the world"* (Matt. 5:14). Jesus shines in the hearts of the saints just as He shines through their faces. Glory to God!

So God is warning you through His saints and getting people ready. He is sending out the warning in every direction, telling people to escape from the city of destruction and not to linger in the plains. Put on your wedding garments, accept the invitation, and get ready to take the flight through the air. When the saints are taken out of the world, there will be no restraining power, and the Devil will be let loose. People will sigh for the days in which we now live, after the Holy Spirit goes up with the body of Christ, the bride. They will sigh and cry, "There is no prophet anymore, no priests. We don't hear from heaven. There is no light; everything is darkness."

There will be awful darkness. The door will be shut, and no one will have an opportunity to join the bride. (See Matthew 25:10.) The bride is being prepared

Some Will Not Taste Death

and adorned now. (See Revelation 21:2.) May God help us to see this. So the message is for you. Some of you here tonight will never experience death until you see the Son of Man coming in the clouds of heaven (Matt. 16:28). Hallelujah! Keep looking up. Are you ready to go? If you are not, come tonight.

The disciples did not understand what Jesus meant when He said, *"There be some standing here, which shall not taste of death, till they see the Son of man coming in his kingdom."* However, He took those who were nearest to Him—those who were watching and praying and looking for those things to come true—He took three of them and slipped away from everybody, and He brought them up into a high mountain. Nobody knew where He was.

That is a good place to be—way up above the world with the Devil under your feet. How beautiful on the mountain are the feet of those who are running up the mountain and hurling down the glad tidings that Jesus is coming! (See Isaiah 52:7.) That is a good place to go in order to pray, if you pray correctly. Bless the Lord, it is not the long prayer or the loud prayer that is effective but, hallelujah, the prayer of faith. Jesus took the disciples up the mountain to pray, and something happened. He had told them, "I am coming in all my Father's glory, and in all the glory of the holy angels, and some of you here are going to see this."

Just before Peter went to be with the Lord, he said, "There will be lying wolves (see 2 Peter 2:1–3), but don't forget what you have heard. I have been telling you that He is coming again, and I have not been telling you *'cunningly devised fables'* (1:16); I am telling you the truth. I saw the King transfigured, and I heard the voice of the great God of heaven. He came down to welcome the bride; He came down to be at the Wedding. The cloud of glory settled over us, and out of that cloud there was a great voice, the voice of God Almighty, and He introduced the bride to His Son: 'This is my Son. He is my Son, the King of Glory. I am pleased at the selection of His bride.'" (See 2 Peter 1:16–18.) Hallelujah!

In the Twinkling of an Eye

The disciples saw the manifestations. They saw Him just exactly as it is going to be when the saints go up. They had the picture, the vision. *"Fear not, little flock"* (Luke 12:32). In that vision, He brought before their eyes the saints who are going up one of these days. There are some living now who will not experience death until they see Jesus come. He brought the picture before them in a vision. Every tribe, tongue, and nation on earth will be in that company, witnesses out of every nation. These three disciples were permitted to see them all changed just like they will be when He comes. We will be all changed: *"We shall not all sleep, but we shall all be changed, in a moment, in the twinkling of an eye"* (1 Cor. 15:51–52). We will have glorious bodies like the Son of God (Phil. 3:21), and *"we shall be like him; for we shall see him as he is"* (1 John 3:2).

Now, then, John saw this picture twice. God has not left us in the dark. John was a man like we are, but God reveals the *"deep things of God"* (1 Cor. 2:10) to His saints. Near the end of his life, John had been banished to the Isle of Patmos. One time, when he was talking to the Lord, the Spirit of God was all over and around him; he saw an open door, and in a minute he was translated to heaven.

Some Will Not Taste Death

He saw the saints go up, and he went up with them. He saw thrones and those who sat upon them, and he saw Christ on the throne of His Father. (See Revelation 4:1–4.) *"To him that overcometh will I grant to sit with me in my throne, even as I also overcame, and am set down with my Father in his throne"* (Rev. 3:21). He overcame the Devil at the very end, and we must not only commence but also go on to the end. When He overcame at the end, He went up, and God gave Him a seat at His right hand—the highest place in the courts of glory—and He is there today. Stephen saw the glory of God, and He saw Jesus standing at the right hand of God in majesty on high. (See Acts 7:55–56.)

"To him that overcometh will I grant to sit with me in my throne, even as I also overcame, and am set down with my Father in his throne." He has not taken His own throne yet.

John saw the saints go up the second time. Then he saw Jesus take His throne, and he went up to the Marriage Supper. *"Blessed are they which are called unto the marriage supper of the Lamb"* (Rev. 19:9). Blessed are they that will eat bread at that Supper and drink wine in my Father's kingdom. (See Matthew 26:29.) We are going to be substantial people, aren't we? Glory to God! Sit down to the Marriage Supper of the Lamb. That is the place He is preparing for you. Oh, glory to God! Don't you want to be there?

We are a nation despised and hated, a *"nation not desired"* (Zeph. 2:1). The Devil hates us, and all his imps hate us. But Jesus says, "Come, hide away. Come together: bind yourselves together and get ready for the *'manifestation of the sons of God'* (Rom. 8:19). *'Fear not, it is your Father's good pleasure to give you the kingdom'*

(Luke 12:32)." He will make us kings and priests in the sight of our God (Rev. 1:6). Kings and priests—glory to God!

So Jesus will come out and take the throne, and the bridal company will be the highest in heaven. There are great degrees of glory, but the overcomers—the bridal party—will sit with Jesus Christ the Lamb of God on His Great White Throne through all the ages. They will follow the Lamb wherever He goes. They are the ones whom Daniel saw: *"They that turn many to righteousness"* will shine as the sun (Dan. 12:3). There are degrees of glory. I would rather be one of the wise ones. (See verse 3.)

The glory of God knocked Paul blind, and it put the noonday sun in the shade. When the saints of God burst forth and their bodies are changed, they will eclipse the sun. Don't you think it will be great? Don't you think you had better advance a degree of glory today?

Jesus said to Peter, James, and John: "Don't tell any man about the vision until after I have gone to glory." (See Matthew 17:9.) So they saw something the rest did not know. This was because they were nearer to God. They wanted God to let them down into the *"deep things of God"* (1 Cor. 2:10). That teaches us a lesson, dear friends. There are degrees of glory. *"They that be wise shall shine as the brightness of the firmament"* (Dan. 12:3); those who are wise will know when Jesus comes.

Do you think that God would not reveal these things to His waiting bride? I tell you, no. We know a few things now. We know it is very soon. "You are not left in the dark; *'ye are all the children of light, and the children of the day'* (1 Thess. 5:5). You have been illuminated from heaven. You will not be overtaken by surprise."

Are we ready? Are we watching? Be ready to stand when the Son of Man comes. Always *"watch and pray"* (Mark 13:33). Watch the signs, and watch the prophecies, so that you may be counted worthy to escape the awful tribulations and stand before the Son of Man when He comes. *"Watch and pray."* You know the signs. You will not be overtaken as by a thief (see 1 Thessalonians 5:2), because I am warning you. You are the *"children of the day,"* and you will know. Glory to God!

So the Lord now shows us all these awful calamities that are coming on the earth. He says, "Do not be fearful when you see these awful things coming. Look up and rejoice. Lift your heads and see the break of day. The sun is rising. Lift up your heads. Rejoice, for *'your redemption draweth nigh'* (Luke 21:28)." Glory!

The secret of the Lord is with those who love Him, those whom He can trust. So God is revealing these things to us from day to day. We will not be surprised. When you see certain signs, know that it is even at your door. We know that now. We don't know the day or hour, but God gives us to understand that we will know a little while before we are taken up. And when you get to the point at which you cannot do anything else, just stand. Wait for the Son of Man to come and catch His waiting bride away.

The Bride Adorned for the Bridegroom

Make sure you understand this: there are great degrees of glory. Don't you want to be the beautiful bride and stand before the King of Glory? Her clothes are so beautiful with fine needlework. (See Psalm 45:14.) And, oh, how she loves her Bridegroom. She doesn't worship anybody but Him. She is not trifling with many lovers, but He has become the "[fairest] *among ten thousand*" (Song 5:10) to her. She is willing to leave all and go with her lover.

Sometimes, when a woman marries a stranger, there is a lot of opposition. Her father says, "If you go, I will disinherit you." But she leaves her parents, her home, and her money. She says, "I love my lover best. He is mine, and I am his. I will have to leave you." So she leaves everything, and she gets into the ship and sails with her strange lover to a strange land where she has never been, among strange people whom she has not known. He is so proud of her, and she is so proud of him. She says, "He is strange to the world, but he is mine, and I am his. I will be glad to go."

There are degrees of glory. God said, "The wise will know." (See Daniel 2:21–22; 12:10.) Don't think it is strange that none of the wicked will know about the coming of the Lord. Daniel saw the saints robed in white on land and sea and God dispersing the Holy Spirit through them. Daniel, one of the wise, will know. God reveals His secrets to the wise. Are you one of the wise? Is God letting you down into the *"deep things"* (1 Cor. 2:10)? Bless God, He will!

We are in the Holy Spirit school, going from one room to another, from one school to another, graduating, getting our diplomas. God wants us to get down into the *"deep things."* He reveals His secrets to us just as He did to Peter, James, and John. He told them, "Don't tell anyone until after I am raised from the dead." It was hidden from the rest. That shows us, dear friends, that there are degrees in glory. Some will shine as stars, and some will eclipse the sun. A great many people will not know when Jesus comes. The wise will know when Jesus comes.

Many people think they will know, but they will be left. God is showing us these things and giving us this lesson. As Jesus told us, there will be two sleeping in one bed; one will be taken, and the other left. There will be two grinding at the mill; one will be taken, and the other left (Luke 17:34–35).

After Jesus was crucified and before His resurrection, the disciples were all in the dark. They lost their faith. In a parallel way, all power will be taken away when Christ is gone and the saints are gone from the earth. The Devil will be let loose, and the Antichrist will begin to show his power.

We find a type of this period in the story of the man who had the demons in him. The disciples could not cast the demons out. The father brought his son to Jesus and said, "The demons try to drown him, burn him, and knock his brains out." Jesus cast the demons out and commanded that they never enter into him any more. (See Matthew 17:14–21.) In the same way, the Antichrist will burn some and drown some and knock the heads off others, as in the dark days. Then Jesus will come back, bind the Devil, and destroy the army of the Antichrist, including two-thirds of all the earth. Only one-third, who went through all the fires trusting God the best they could, are going to escape.

Chapter 16

The Resurrection of the Saints

Thou hast ascended on high, thou hast led captivity captive: thou hast received gifts for men; yea, for the rebellious also, that the LORD God might dwell among them.
—Psalm 68:18

After all the life of Jesus—after all His mighty signs and wonders and miracles, after people exclaimed, *"Behold the man!"* (John 19:5), *"Never man spake like this man"* (John 7:46), and *"What manner of man is this, that even the winds and the sea obey him!"* (Matt. 8:27)—after all this, if He had stopped short at Calvary or at going down into the cold grave, His work would have been a failure. Many people only see a dead Savior. They only have a dead religion of form and works. They have no life or power.

At the end of the Old Testament, Israel had forsaken the Lord, and He had taken His Spirit from her. For about four hundred years, she was in darkness. There were no prophets or priests. There was no communication from heaven, until the birth of John the Baptist and the birth of Christ were announced.

Remember that Jesus brought *"life and immortality to light"* (2 Tim. 1:10)—to us—through the Resurrection. No, the grave could not hold Him, though all hell was up in arms to try to hold Him cold in death. A hundred or more armed soldiers stood around His grave, for fear that His disciples would steal His lifeless body away. They also sealed the sepulcher with the governor's seal, and it was death to break that seal. (See Matthew 27:64–66.)

A mighty battle was fought. All the armies of heaven were engaged with the hosts of hell in fierce array around the rock casket or tomb where the mangled body of Jesus, our crucified Lord, lay cold in death. Hear the demons: "We have got Him, and we will hold Him captive. Where is your Prince? Where is your King?" But listen! The battle is turning; victory is near; help is coming. The Lord God Almighty Himself is coming with His great angel who rolls back the stone from the sepulcher and sits upon it. The Bible tells us that *"his countenance was like lightning, and his raiment white as snow: and for fear of him the keepers did shake"* (Matt. 28:3–4). They fell and lay as dead men.

God, with His mighty presence, sent a great earthquake. With a great shout over death and hell and the grave, we see the Conqueror come forth, holding the keys to unlock the prison house of the dead.

We see the women who were the last at the cross and the first at the grave. The angel said,

> *Fear not ye: for I know that ye seek Jesus, which was crucified. He is not here: for he is risen, as he*

*said. Come, see the place where the Lord lay. And go
quickly, and tell his disciples that he is risen from the
dead.*   (Matt. 28:5–7)

As they went with great joy, Jesus met them, saying,
"Fear not, but go and tell my brothers that I will meet
them in Galilee." (See verse 10.)

The women were commanded by the angels, and
later by the Lord Himself, to preach the first news of
the Resurrection.

No, He is not dead. *"The Lord is risen indeed"* (Luke
24:34). Oh, praise God for a living Christ, a living
church, and our soon-coming King and Lord!

After His resurrection, the graves were opened, and
many of the bodies of the saints that slept in their graves
arose, came out, went into the city, and appeared to
many. (See Matthew 27:52–53.) The Scripture says, *"And
many bodies of the saints which slept arose"* (v. 52). The
word *many* here implies thousands or more, and I believe
that most of those saints were the prophets and priests:
Abraham, Isaac, Jacob, and Joseph, in addition to those
holy men of old who spoke as they were moved by the
Holy Spirit (2 Pet. 1:21), including John the Baptist, who
had recently been murdered for Jesus' sake.

Oh, praise God for the resurrection of these mighty
men of old! Their bodies came up, and their spirits
were united to them. They were living men; they were
breathing and walking, and their bodies were free
from corruption. See them going through the streets
of Jerusalem, going from one place to another and
making themselves known.

Oh, praise God for the resurrection of our bodies!
Praise God that we will know each other!

Yes, the Devil held their bodies captive for hundreds of years in the grave. But see the mighty Conqueror break the chains, take them captive from the Devil and from the power of the grave, and—leading *"captivity captive"* (Eph. 4:8)—lead them away to some other world, where no doubt God is using them in some great way for His glory.

"Gifts to Men"

Jesus ascended on high and gave gifts to men (Eph. 4:8). Yes, He gave them even to the rebels, also. Jesus did not have *"all power"* (Matt. 28:18) until after God raised Him from the dead. No one could have the gift of God, eternal life, until after he was *"born of the Spirit"* (John 3:6).

Jesus has all power. He was raised up with all power. (See Romans 1:4.) The Holy Spirit was with the disciples, but Jesus said, *"The Spirit of truth…shall be in you"* (John 14:17). When the disciples were all together, Jesus met with them, and He opened their spiritual minds. He breathed on them and said, *"Receive ye the Holy Ghost"* (John 20:22). They received Him and became *"partakers of the divine nature"* (2 Pet. 1:4). They received the gift of God, were enlightened, and cried out, with Thomas, *"My Lord and my God"* (John 20:28). No one had ever had that experience before that time. They were sons of God by the new birth. It was the gift of God, eternal life. Yes, *"for the rebellious also."* This is the most important of all gifts, for without this gift you can never get inside the pearly gates.

When the sinner stops his rebellion, and repents, God gives him faith to accept Christ. God gives him power to become a son of God who is born not of man or of the will of men, not of flesh and blood, but by the power of God. (See John 1:12–13.) He is then no longer a rebel but a son, for he has received the gift of God and has been born of the spiritual family of God. His name has been written in the family record by the finger of God, and it has been said, "This man was born in Zion." (See Psalm 87:5.) The finished work on Calvary atones for his sin and uncleanness, and he is now a child of God, ready for any or all of the gifts of the Pentecostal baptism and power. He is God's man.

Jesus received gifts for men (Eph. 4:8). When He was giving His last blessing to His disciples on the mountain before going up to heaven, He said the following to them:

Tarry ye in the city of Jerusalem, until ye be endued with power from on high.   (Luke 24:49)

But ye shall receive power, after that the Holy Ghost is come upon you: and ye shall be witnesses unto me.
                                                      (Acts 1:8)

All power is given unto me in heaven and in earth.
                                                      (Matt. 28:18)

Go ye into all the world, and preach the gospel to every creature....These signs shall follow them that believe [in Me]; in my name shall they cast out devils; they shall speak with new tongues; they shall take up serpents; and if they drink any deadly thing, it shall not hurt them; they shall lay hands on the sick, and they shall recover.   (Mark 16:15, 17–18)

The Holy Spirit

In this last Scripture, Jesus was saying to His disciples, in effect, "These are some of the gifts that I will give to men."

These were the last words our Savior spoke on earth before He was taken up out of the disciples' sight in a visible manner. After that, they got the promised baptism and greatest gift; they went forth preaching the Word everywhere, *"the Lord working with them, and confirming the word with signs following"* (Mark 16:20).

The disciples could not see the Lord in person as in days past, but they saw the visible signs of His invisible presence. These signs and gifts could be seen and heard with the natural eye and ear. Jesus was with them, with all gifts, signs, miracles, and diverse operations of the Spirit. With these, He confirmed and put His seal on the truth and on their preaching.

At Pentecost, He sent the *"promise of the Father"* (Acts 1:4). The Holy Spirit came as a *"rushing mighty wind"* and sat on all their heads like *"cloven tongues...of fire"* (Acts 2:2–3). These cloven tongues were a sign of the new tongues; they were tongues of fire and of the Spirit, for all the disciples were filled with the Spirit and began to speak *"as the Spirit gave them utterance"* (v. 4).

It was at the time of the great Jewish Feast of Pentecost, and Jewish people from *"every nation under heaven"* (v. 5) were gathered there. They saw and heard the wonderful demonstration of the Holy Spirit, the gifts, and the glory of God. They were amazed, saying, "What does this mean? *'How hear we every man in our own tongue, wherein we were born?'* (v. 8)." Jesus had sent down gifts for men and women. The Holy Spirit had come to stay. He was given now without measure. (See John 3:34.)

The Resurrection of the Saints

In the book of Acts, we read that God sent Peter down to Caesarea to hold a revival among the Gentiles. While he was preaching, the Holy Spirit fell on those who heard the Word, for they spoke with tongues and magnified God. (See Acts 10.)

The Holy Spirit, with all the accompanying gifts, was poured out on the Gentile nations, just as He had been poured out on the Jews at Pentecost. *"For the promise is unto you, and to your children, and to all that are afar off, even as many as the Lord our God shall call"* (Acts 2:39). Praise God, beloved, for that includes you and me!

Jesus sent these gifts with all the Pentecostal power and glory. Our bodies are God's power plants; they are channels for the Holy Spirit to flow out of like *"rivers of living water"* (John 7:38). In reference to this *"living water,"* the Scriptures tell us, *"This spake he of the Spirit, which they that believe on him should receive"* (v. 39).

Signs of His Presence

Thou hast ascended on high, thou hast led captivity captive: thou hast received gifts for men; yea, for the rebellious also, that the LORD God might dwell among them.

This is the evidence to the lost world that God is with us: the signs of His invisible presence. We are a people to be wondered at. "Father, here am I, and the children whom You have given." (See John 17:9–11, 24.) God's purpose is that we would work signs and wonders in Israel from the Lord of Hosts, who dwells in Zion (Isa. 8:18)—down here, not in heaven. *"He led captivity captive, and gave gifts unto men....He gave some, apostles;*

and some, prophets; and some, evangelists; and some, pastors and teachers" (Eph. 4:8, 11). These imply and include all the gifts and workings of the Holy Spirit.

Why did He send this power and these gifts to men—to His disciples and to the church? *"For the perfecting of the saints, for the work of the ministry, for the edifying of the body of Christ"* (v. 12). Christ gave gifts in order to make the saints, God's men, perfect and to lead them in the same Pentecostal power and gifts.

Ministers need the power of God, and they must have the seal of the Holy Spirit, with all these signs and gifts, to encourage them. Not only are these signs and gifts God's seal to them, but they are also the visible signs to the world that God is with His people, working together with them, confirming the Word with visible signs (Mark 16:20).

When the disciples were put into prison and their lives were threatened on account of the great power that was with them in healing and miracles, they were forbidden to preach in the name of Jesus, for the authorities saw that the power came through His name. (See Acts 4:1–21.)

The disciples met together, and they knew that the demonstration of the power of God had caused all their persecution. They knew that if they had a form of religion but denied the power (see 2 Timothy 3:5), they would have no more trouble with the authorities. But, beloved, they said, "We will be true to God. We will preach the Word if we die." Then they prayed to the Lord, saying,

Lord, behold their threatenings: and grant unto thy servants, that with all boldness they may speak thy

word, by stretching forth thine hand to heal; and that signs and wonders may be done by the name of thy holy child Jesus. (Acts 4:29–30)

You see that these ministers needed power to give them boldness to stand up for Jesus, to preach *"all the words of this life"* (Acts 5:20).

When they preached, they knew they must see in their meetings the signs of the presence of the invisible Christ, who would be present to confirm the Word and their message. Jesus had said, *"I am with you alway, even unto the end of the world"* (Matt. 28:20). With the signs of Christ's presence, they could say to the people, like Peter had at Pentecost, "What you see and hear and feel is the promise of the Father; it is the Holy Spirit." (See Acts 2:33.)

The Son was pleased with the disciples' prayer (see Acts 4:29–30) and with their faith and courage, and the building where they were assembled was shaken. They were all filled with the Holy Spirit and spoke the Word with boldness (v. 31).

See, beloved, this was a greater baptism. They needed it to prepare them for the work they had to do. After this, they had greater success. God did mighty signs and wonders through the apostles; great fear fell on all the church and on all who heard and saw these things. *"Multitudes both of men and women"* (Acts 5:14) came flocking to Christ and were added to the Lord. (See verses 11–14.)

"Multitudes" means thousands. They came from Jerusalem and all the surrounding cities, bringing their sick folk on beds and cots and placing them along the streets so that the shadow of Peter passing by might fall

on them (vv. 15–16). You see that the power went forth from the disciples' bodies. The same thing happened when handkerchiefs that had touched Paul's body were sent to the sick; the devils or diseases went out, and people were healed (Acts 19:11–12).

Oh, praise God, I am a witness to these things! We see the same thing today: some of the greatest miracles of healing and salvation I have ever seen have been done in the same way, hundreds of miles away. He *"gave gifts unto men"* (Eph. 4:8).

Read carefully the twelfth chapter of the first epistle to the Corinthians. Paul showed that the church is in possession of all the gifts, power, calling, and work of the Holy Spirit; they are in the body of Christ, His church.

Oh, beloved, we ought to live in this way, in all places, in these last days when the bride is making herself ready (Rev. 19:7). Paul said he did not want us to be ignorant concerning spiritual gifts (1 Cor. 12:1). *"Covet earnestly the best gifts"* (v. 31). *"Follow after charity* [love], *and desire spiritual gifts"* (14:1), for God has set them in the church.

Gifts are *"for the rebellious also."* Thank God, the sinner no longer needs to be rebellious. He can fall at God's feet and settle the old account. God says He has a gift for you. Oh, *"the gift of God is eternal life"* (Rom. 6:23). When you receive this gift, then you are God's man. You are no longer a stranger or foreigner, but have been brought near by the blood of Christ. Through Him, you will have access to the Father by one Spirit. You are a citizen with the saints and of the household of God; you are a living stone (1 Peter 2:5 NKJV) in the building that is being fitly framed together, a holy temple in the Lord. (See Ephesians 2:12–22.)

The Resurrection of the Saints

Beloved, you are a son and an heir to all the Pentecostal blessings, gifts, and power. Press your claims at the court of heaven. Seek the baptism of the Holy Spirit and power. You can be a *"pillar in the temple of...God"* (Rev. 3:12). You will go in, and will go out no more (v. 12).

Let all who read this take warning: "He who knows My will and does not do it, will be beaten with many lashes." (See Luke 12:47.) Be among the wise who will know of the Lord's coming, the wise who will *"shine as the brightness of the firmament"* (Dan. 12:3).

Chapter 17

The Marriage Supper of the Lamb

Blessed are they which are called unto the marriage supper of the Lamb.
—Revelation 19:9

Oh, beloved, have you been called? Let us be glad and rejoice and give honor to Him, for the Marriage of the Lamb has come. The bride must be arrayed in linen, pure and white.

Yes, His wife has made herself ready; see the King coming out of His ivory palace, which He has made ready to receive His bride. His garments are overflowing with sweet scents. They smell of *"myrrh, and aloes, and cassia"* (Ps. 45:8).

The bride is rejoicing in His love. Listen, O daughters! Beloved, are we the blessed who are called to the banquet, to this heavenly Marriage Supper in the skies? Oh, consider, and incline your ears to hear the whispers of His love. We must forget our own people and our Father's house (v. 10). Our beloved Bridegroom is very jealous. We must love Him with our whole heart and our whole being. We must long for Him, so that He will greatly desire our beauty. He is our Lord, and we must worship Him (Ps 45:11).

We must be ready to leave all at any moment when the herald shouts, "Behold the Bridegroom. Behold, He comes; go forth to meet Him." (See Matthew 25:6.) Oh, are you ready to leave all to sail away with our Beloved to that heavenly kingdom, to those mansions in the City of Gold that He has been preparing and adorning for so many years with all the wealth and jewels of heaven? Oh, that City of Gold!

Do our hearts leap for joy? Do we cry, "Come, oh, come quickly, my Redeemer, my Beloved, and my King"? Oh, Most Mighty, with Your glory and Your majesty, You are fairer than all the sons of men! *"Thy throne, O God, is for ever and ever: the sceptre of thy kingdom is a right sceptre"* (v. 6).

Oh, look at the lovely bride. They are all honorable women—kings' daughters. Behold, on His right hand stands the queen robed in the shining glory of Ophir. (See verse 9.)

> *The king's daughter is all glorious within: her cloth-ing is of wrought gold. She shall be brought unto the king in raiment of needlework: the virgins her com-panions that follow her shall be brought unto thee.*
> (vv. 13–14)

Oh, glory to God! Look at the virgins, the guests at the wedding. They will go in with gladness; they will be brought into the King's palace, rejoicing with great joy (v. 15).

The Marriage Supper of the Lamb

Streets like Transparent Glass

Oh, the very gates of solid pearl! The walls are jasper and the city is pure gold, like clear glass. The streets are pure gold, like transparent glass. The very foundations are built and *"garnished with all manner of precious stones"* (Rev. 21:19; see also verses 18–21).

Oh, behold! Let us rise on the wings of faith and in the Spirit take a view of our eternal home. *"The city is laid out as a square"* (Rev. 21:16 NKJV). It is fifteen hundred miles long, fifteen hundred miles wide, and fifteen hundred miles high. Oh, those pearly gates and jasper walls! How they shine in the glorious brightness and light of God and of the Lamb. Oh, beloved, if the outside is so glorious, what will it be like to live in the city, to roam through the courts of glory?

Our Lord says that we will go in with joy and rejoicing. (See Psalm 45:15.) Oh, our Lord will have many surprises for us as He takes us through our beautiful mansions. We will sit with Him on His throne (Rev. 3:21) and be surrounded with all the brightness and glory of heaven.

We will see the River of Life running out from beneath the throne of God, like a sea of clear glass (Rev. 22:1). There will be the nation of kings, with their gold-crowned heads. (See Revelation 4:4.)

We will eat of the Tree of Life that bears twelve kinds of fruits every month (Rev. 22:2). Oh, this beautiful tree on each side of the River! We will eat of its fruit.

Jesus said, *"I say unto you, I will not drink henceforth of this fruit of the vine, until that day when I drink it new with you in my Father's kingdom"* (Matt. 26:29). Yes, we will eat and drink with our Bridegroom in His kingdom. Jesus said, *"I appoint unto you a kingdom, as my Father hath appointed unto me; that ye may eat and drink at my table in my kingdom"* (Luke 22:29–30). Oh, praise the Lord, this is strong proof that the kingdom is literal and natural. And it will be free from the curse of sin. *"Blessed are they which are called unto the marriage supper of the Lamb."*

See the Feast: the Lord will *"make…a feast of fat things, a feast of wines on the lees, of fat things full of marrow, of wines on the lees well refined"* (Isa. 25:6). He will swallow up death in victory (1 Cor. 15:54). And the Lord God Himself will wipe all tears from all faces (Rev. 7:17). The rebuke will be forever taken off His people.

Oh, hasten the day when the kingdoms of this world will become the kingdoms of our Lord and of His Christ. He will reign, and we will reign with Him for the ages of ages. (See Revelation 11:15; 22:5.) Oh, blessed King, come and take up Your great power, and reign!

We now bear the image of Adam, the first man, but our fleshly bodies will be changed and made *"like unto his glorious body"* (Phil. 3:21). Our mortal bodies will be changed into immortal bodies (1 Cor. 15:53–54). In the same body He had before His crucifixion, Jesus ate fish with His disciples after He rose from the dead; it will be the same with us, for *"we shall be like him"* (1 John 3:2). Our bodies will be resurrected or translated and glorified.

Beloved, *"we shall not all sleep, but we shall all be changed, in a moment, in the twinkling of an eye"* (1 Cor. 15:51–52). *"Then we which are alive and remain shall be caught up together with them* [the risen and glorified dead] *in the clouds, to meet the Lord in the air: and so shall we ever be with the Lord"* (1 Thess. 4:17).

The time is about up: Jesus will come to take out a people to be His bride and will give her His name. Yes, we will be called the bride, the Lamb's wife; she will be His pride and glory. He will be glorified in her through the ages of the ages.

As they travel through the many beautiful worlds, He will present her, in all her beauty; and she, in her pride and glory, will point to her royal Bridegroom and tell of His wonderful redeeming love.

The Time Is at Hand

Yes, the time is at hand. Jesus has given us many signs so that we would know when to look for His return, so that we would know that His coming is near, *"even at the doors"* (Matt. 24:33). He said that the wise would know (Dan. 12:10). *"And they that be wise shall shine as the brightness of the firmament"* (v. 3).

Oh, beloved, are we watching? Are we waiting? Will we be ready to escape all the awful things that are coming on the earth? To many who are looking, it will be a day of darkness, and there will be no light in it for them. He will come as suddenly as a flash of lightning, and we will be taken as quickly.

He will come with all the brightness of heaven. The saints will see all His glory and will hear all the bells of heaven ringing. Amid the singing of the great angelic choir, they will be caught away, swallowed up in all this brightness and glory. But the poor lost world will sleep on, not knowing what has happened. Remember, two will be sleeping in one bed; one will be taken, and the other will be left to sleep on. Two will be at the mill, grinding; one will be taken, the other left. Two will be in the field; one will be taken, the other left. (See Luke 17:34–36.)

So suddenly will this appear that they will not know it until it is too late. Then they will realize what has happened, when they see that all these foolish "fanatics," these people, have disappeared.

No, the world is too blinded in darkness and sin. She cannot behold the glory of the Rapture as the saints go shouting through the air.

Hark! We can almost hear them marshaling the hosts of heaven, the angels tuning their harps of gold. We can almost see the Banquet, the table spread for the Marriage Supper in the air. Many have seen the table, reaching across the skies. The great preparation is soon coming. Oh, dear reader, will you accept the invitation to the Marriage Supper in the skies? Oh, glory to God, I will meet you there!

Chapter 18

Christ and His Bride

The apostle Paul wrote that Christ *"loved the church, and gave himself for it"* (Eph. 5:25) so that she might be *"a glorious church, not having spot, or wrinkle, or any such thing; but that it should be holy and without blemish"* (v. 27).

She must be a glorious church, not having *"spot, or wrinkle"* or any such thing. She must be *"holy and without blemish."* Oh, beloved, it means much to be a member of this church. Let us now see how the church is to be the bride of Christ.

In the third chapter of Revelation, Jesus Himself gave John a description of the Philadelphian church, whose name signifies love:

And to the angel of the church in Philadelphia write: These things saith he that is holy, he that is true, he that hath the key of David, he that openeth, and no man shutteth; and shutteth, and no man openeth; I know thy works: behold, I have set before thee an open door, and no man can shut it: for thou hast a little strength, and hast kept my word, and hast not denied my name. Behold, I will make them of the synagogue of Satan, which say they are Jews, and are not, but do lie; behold, I will make them to come and worship before thy feet, and to know that I have loved thee. Because thou hast kept the word of my patience, I also will keep thee from the hour of temptation, which shall come upon all the world, to try them that dwell upon the earth. Behold, I come quickly: hold that fast which thou hast, that no man take thy crown. Him that overcometh will I make a pillar in the temple of my God, and he shall go no more out: and I will write upon him the name of my God, and the name of the city of my God, which is new Jerusalem, which cometh down out of heaven from my God: and I will write upon him my new name. (Rev. 3:7–12)

The book of Revelation, attributed to the apostle John, is the most wonderful book of the New Testament. Peter once asked Jesus about John's future: *"And what shall this man do?"* (John 21:21). Jesus had answered Peter, *"If I will that he tarry till I come, what is that to thee? follow thou me"* (v. 22). After that, the report went out that John would never die.

Tradition says that when John was quite old, the enemies of Christ tried to kill him. They threw him into a kettle of boiling oil, but the Lord did not let it hurt him. Then his enemies were frightened; they banished him to the lonely island called Patmos, and he was left there to die. He had been such a true witness for Jesus and His Word that it was the darkest hour of his life, but he was alone with God, filled with the Spirit.

As I said, the book of Revelation is a wonderful book. About sixty-four years after John and the other disciples saw Jesus go up to heaven, Christ came back to earth and appeared to John. He gave John great, moving pictures of the church, starting from the Day of Pentecost.

Oh, what power! What a force! What a light He brought to John in those dark days in which the church then lived! *"All things are possible to him that believeth"* (Mark 9:23).

Jesus came back to John in all His kingly power and glory. He had been gone a long time. The change was so great, and John felt so little in His presence, that when he saw Him, he *"fell at his feet as dead"* (Rev. 1:17). John said that Jesus laid His right hand on him, saying, *"'Fear not...I am alive for evermore'"* (vv. 17–18). John, do you know me? We fished together, walked together, and slept together. Many times you have rested your weary head on my chest."

Can you imagine the joy John experienced when he heard the familiar voice of the Galilean, which had quieted the disciples' fears so often, when the sweet voice said, "It is I; do not be afraid. I have come back to bring you important messages. I want you to write all you hear, and send it to the churches"?

The first three chapters of Revelation give the history of Christ's body, or church, from the time she was established at Pentecost down to the last believer who overcomes, and on to the close, where the church is taken up to glory and seated on the throne with Jesus, executing judgment on the lost world. These chapters also show all that will take place through the end of Christ's thousand-year reign. (See Revelation 20:4.)

The first thing John heard was a loud voice that sounded like a trumpet. He looked to where the voice came from, and he saw seven golden candlesticks, representing the seven churches, or types of Christians, down to the last. He saw Jesus in the midst of the candlesticks, in all His power and glory. His eyes were like a blaze of fire, His feet like a blazing furnace. His voice was like the sound of many waters. In His right hand were seven stars. Out of His mouth came a two-edged sword. His countenance was like the sun, shining in all its strength. (See Revelation 1:10–16.) Oh, glory to God! What a Prince! What a King! What a living, wonder-working power is our Christ in His church. He is in us, beneath us, around us, like a wall of fire!

He shows us that our greatest trials and battles will be with the Devil in the enemies of Christ who are also the enemies of His true church. But hear Him say, "Behold, I will make them come and fall at our feet and acknowledge that God loves us and that we are His true witnesses." (See Revelation 3:9.)

Today, Christ is on trial for His honor and glory as never before. When so-called "great preachers" are denying the atoning blood of Christ and everything except the dead letter of the law (see Romans 7:6), hear Him say, "I hold the key. I will open for you." No man or power can close the door against us. We will keep His Word and not deny His name or be ashamed of His works. (See Revelation 3:7–8.)

He warns us that we will have trouble. We will be persecuted. We will be misrepresented by false prophets who call themselves *"Jews"*—or, in today's terms, "great Christians" and "leaders"—but who are of the *"synagogue of Satan"* (Rev. 2:9), who lie, and who do not practice the truth (v. 9; see also 1 John 1:6).

Come out of the "Laodicean" church, which represents spiritual lukewarmness, and become a "Philadelphian." (See Revelation 3:7–12; 14–21.)

Christ and His Bride

The Rapture of the Saints

The fourth chapter of Revelation shows the Rapture of the saints and that their seat is on Christ's throne. All through the book of Revelation, Jesus describes the condition of the church, and His message still applies to us who are living on earth today.

The Laodicean church is the last, or great, church of today; it includes all organizations or groups in the world having a nice *"form of godliness, but denying the power thereof: from such turn away"* (2 Tim. 3:5). There has been a falling away from the doctrine of Christ and from the Holy Spirit, apostolic power, and wisdom, to a cold formality and to a teaching of the *"tradition*[s]*"* and *"doctrines of men"* (Col. 2:8, 22).

And unto the angel of the church of the Laodiceans write; These things saith the Amen, the faithful and true witness, the beginning of the creation of God; I know thy works, that thou art neither cold nor hot: I would thou wert cold or hot. So then because thou art lukewarm, and neither cold nor hot, I will spue thee out of my mouth. Because thou sayest, I am rich, and increased with goods, and have need of nothing; and knowest not that thou art wretched, and miserable, and poor, and blind, and naked: I counsel thee to buy of me gold tried in the fire, that thou mayest be rich; and white raiment, that thou mayest be clothed, and that the shame of thy nakedness do not appear; and anoint thine eyes with eyesalve, that thou mayest see. As many as I love, I rebuke and chasten: be zealous therefore, and repent. Behold, I stand at the door, and knock: if any man hear my voice, and open the

door, I will come in to him, and will sup with him,
and he with me. To him that overcometh will I grant
to sit with me in my throne, even as I also overcame,
and am set down with my Father in his throne. He
that hath an ear, let him hear what the Spirit saith
unto the churches. (Rev. 3:14–22)

This is what concerns us. God is calling His people out of the Laodicean church. Thousands have heard the call: *"Come out of her, my people, that ye be not partakers of her sins, and that ye receive not of her plagues"* (Rev. 18:4). The last call is going forth. The Lord is shouting in a voice of thunder through His bride, "Come out quickly." You may have time to be an overcomer *"in the temple of my God"* (Rev. 3:12). Of such He says, *"He shall go no more out"* (v. 12).

The High Rank of the Family of God

The bride must graduate in the highest honors of the Holy Spirit. Those who sit on His throne will be the highest rank of the whole family of God. They will be *"heirs of God, and joint-heirs with Christ"* (Rom. 8:17); they will have kingly power with Christ to rule the nations for one thousand years. They are called the *"wise"* and are those whom Daniel saw: *"And they that be wise shall shine as the brightness of the firmament; and they that turn many to righteousness as the stars for ever and ever"* (Dan. 12:3).

The *"wise shall shine as the brightness of the firmament"* or *"as the stars for ever."* There are degrees of glory: one for the sun, another for the moon (1 Cor. 15:41). We thought years ago that the winning of souls was the greatest work. *"They that turn many to righteousness* [will shine] *as the stars for ever and ever.* However, *"the wise shall shine as the brightness of the firmament."* They will *"shine forth as the sun in the kingdom of their Father"* (Matt. 13:43).

None of the wicked will know anything about when Jesus comes, but the wise will know. Hear Jesus shout, *"To him that overcometh will I grant to sit with me in my throne, even as I also overcame, and am set down with my Father in his throne"* (Rev. 3:21). Oh, praise the Lord! The wise will sit with Christ on His throne.

The wise will know just when Jesus will come for His bride. They will be pillars in His temple (v. 12), in His body, or church. They will be initiated into the *"deep things of God"* (1 Cor. 2:10), and they will know His secrets. They will go in, never to go out. Oh, let us be sure that we are faithful and true. Then He will save us in that hour of trial, or tribulation, that is coming on all the world.

He Himself will come to take His bride, to take us, if we are part of His bride, to the Marriage Supper of the Lamb in the skies. He says, "I am coming quickly," meaning "soon" (Rev. 22:7). Hold fast to all you have received until He comes. See that no man takes your crown. *"Him that overcometh will I make a pillar in* [My church]*"* (Rev. 3:12).

"Watch and pray" (Mark 13:33) so that you may be counted worthy to escape all these things that are coming on the earth and to stand before the Lord.

A Royal Nation in Royal Robes

We are strangers in a strange land (see Exodus 2:22), but we are princes in disguise; our royal robes shine, but the world cannot see them. They cannot see the table our Father has prepared for us, spread out in shining brightness and snowy whiteness. It is covered with royal delicacies: rich wine to make us glad, meat to make us strong, heavenly bread to keep us alive forevermore, and oil to make us shine as bright lights in this dark world.

Our enemies cannot taste of the feast. Oh, praise the Lord, He is calling out a people for a special purpose in these last days. He calls them the wise ones, a chosen generation, a nation called out from among the nations, a royal kingly nation or nation of kings, a holy priesthood, a special people, who confess that they are not of this world, for our citizenship and kingdom are not of this world. (See Daniel 12:3, 10; 1 Peter 2:9; John 18:36.) We confess that we are pilgrims and strangers in this world (Heb. 11:13).

As living stones, we are being built up into a spiritual house (1 Pet. 2:5). Oh, glory to God! We are God's temple, in which He lives and moves. He molds us as clay in order to show His glorious presence, and so the world can see that the treasure is in our earthen vessels and that it is all of God (2 Cor. 4:7).

We are a holy priesthood so that we may offer up spiritual sacrifices to God through Jesus Christ. We are a living church, a spiritual body of Jesus, the living Head. Christ is the Head, and we are the living members of His body.

Christ is the Firstborn. It has pleased God, through Jesus, the Captain of our salvation (Heb. 2:10), to bring many sons and daughters into the kingdom, for He does not call us servants but sons (Gal. 4:7). Because we are the sons of God, He *"hath sent forth the Spirit of his Son into* [our] *hearts, crying, Abba, Father"* (v. 6).

The church of God and of our Lord Jesus Christ was set up in a blaze of glory on the Day of Pentecost. It was built on the foundation laid by the apostles and prophets, Jesus Christ being the Cornerstone (Eph. 2:20). The disciples were the one hundred and twenty "pillars" (Rev. 3:12) who were present at Pentecost and received the Pentecostal baptism. The three thousand who were saved, who received the gift of the Holy Spirit that day, became *"living stones"* (1 Pet. 2:5 NKJV) and were placed in God's building.

The Marriage of the Lamb

"And his wife hath made herself ready....Blessed are they which are called unto the marriage supper of the Lamb" (Rev. 19:7, 9). Psalm 45 tells us,

Kings' daughters [will be] *among* [His] *honourable women: upon* [His] *right hand* [will] *stand the queen in gold of Ophir....The king's daughter is all glorious within: her clothing is of wrought gold.* (vv. 9, 13)

Oh, hear the shouts around the throne, from one end to the other, as *"the voice of a great multitude, and as the voice of many waters, and as the voice of mighty thunderings,* [shouting] *Alleluia: for the Lord God omnipotent reigneth"* (Rev. 19:6). Beloved, what is all this about? Do we comprehend that we are causing all this rejoicing?

All heaven is waiting to hear the shout, "Go forth to meet her." Something wonderful is going to take place soon. The Mighty God, who inhabits eternity, and all the heavenly hosts have been waiting thousands of years for this great event: for the mystical body to come together—Christ our living Head, and the bride, the living body—for the Marriage of the Son of God, the Great Jehovah. *"For the marriage of the Lamb is come"* (Rev. 19:7).

Oh, dearly beloved, let us *"abstain from fleshly lusts, which war against the soul"* (1 Pet. 2:11). Let our words be few and well chosen; let our conversation be in heaven (Phil. 3:20), from which we are expecting a message from the King, telling us that He is coming. We can almost hear the bugle call of the angels, getting the armies of heaven ready for marching; we can almost hear the angelic choir, tuning their harps of gold. All heaven is getting excited.

"To him that overcometh will I grant to sit with me in my throne, even as I also overcame, and am set down with my Father in his throne" (Rev. 3:21). Jesus has not yet taken His throne, and He will not do so until He takes up His bride.

This promise is only to the wise of the bridal party. Those who will sit with Christ on His throne will have the highest rank of all the hosts of heaven. This is only promised to the overcomers in the last days, to those who will be taken up from among men. This is the close of the bride's tenure on earth.

In the first verse of Revelation chapter 4, we see a picture of the church's translation to heaven. John was carried to heaven; he represents the Rapture:

> *Immediately I was in the spirit* [or changed, as we will be in the twinkling of an eye]; *and, behold, a*

> *throne was set in heaven, and one sat on the throne.*
> *And he that sat was to look upon like a jasper...and*
> *there was a rainbow round about the throne.*
>
> (vv. 2–3)

The brightest jewels are mentioned to help us to comprehend a little of the brightness and splendor of the glory of Christ and His bride.

John saw Jesus taking His throne and seating the bride with Him in the midst of the throne:

> *And out of the throne proceeded lightnings and thun-*
> *derings and voices: and there were seven lamps of fire*
> *burning before the throne, which are the seven Spirits*
> *of God. And before the throne there was a sea of glass*
> *like unto crystal: and in the midst of the throne, and*
> *round about the throne, were four beasts full of eyes*
> *before and behind.*   (Rev. 4:5–6)

The Glory of the Bride

The description of these beasts is symbolic of power, the wings and the eyes signifying that they are full of light, power, and knowledge. They are so swallowed up in the sunlight of glory that their crowns cannot be seen.

Now these are not beasts, but the overcomers, shining as the brightness of the sun, seated with Christ on His throne, just like He promised. We see the twenty-four crowned heads seated around the throne, as if in council; yet they are not on the throne (v. 4). We hear these overcomers shouting the loudest praises to the Lamb and to the Lord God Almighty, who was and is and who has come to take His great power and to reign. (See verse 8.)

When the overcomers give glory to Him who sits on the throne, *"who liveth for ever and ever"* (v. 9), they do not fall down, but the twenty-four elders fall before the throne and worship Him, casting their crowns at His feet, saying, *"Thou art worthy, O Lord, to receive glory and honour and power"* (v. 11). You see that the beasts or overcomers on the throne do not fall down; the others fall down in honor of what the living creatures are saying.

However, in Revelation 5:8–10, we read:

> *And when he had taken the book, the four beasts and four and twenty elders fell down before the Lamb, having every one of them harps, and golden vials full of odours, which are the prayers of saints. And they sung a new song, saying, Thou art worthy to take the book, and to open the seals thereof: for thou wast slain, and hast redeemed us to God by thy blood out of every kindred, and tongue, and people, and nation; and hast made us unto our God kings and priests: and we shall reign on the earth.*

You see here that the living creatures, that is, the overcomers, and elders all fall down before the Lamb, *"having every one of them harps, and golden vials full of odours, which are the prayers of saints."* Oh, hear again the shouts of the overcomers with the elders:

> *Thou art worthy...for thou wast slain, and hast redeemed us to God by thy blood out of every kindred, and tongue, and people, and nation; and hast made us unto our God kings and priests: and we shall reign on the earth.*

Christ and His Bride

In Revelation 5:13, we hear all the hosts of heaven and earth raise a shout, giving glory to Him who sits on the throne. The four living creatures say, *"Amen"* (v. 14). Then *"the four and twenty elders [fall] down and [worship] him that liveth for ever and ever"* (v. 14).

When the overcomers say *"Amen,"* the elders fall down and worship, but the living creatures do not fall down, showing that they were redeemed by His blood from all nations and are clothed with the highest honor and power. They are *"joint-heirs with Christ"* (Rom. 8:17) in power and glory.

In Revelation 6, you see the living creatures, the overcomers, on the throne with Christ, executing judgments on the earth during the Great Tribulation. As one after another shouts, *"Come and see"* (Rev. 6:1), one judgment after another comes on the earth.

"'Do ye not know that the saints shall judge the world' (1 Cor. 6:2) and that the saints will judge fallen angels?" (See verse 3.) They will come back with Christ to fight the last great battle when the Antichrist and all his army will be destroyed. After this, they will reign as kings and priests for one thousand years (Rev. 20:6), when all the remnant of men will seek after the Lord and all the Gentiles will call on His name. Oh, hasten the day when the knowledge of God will cover the earth, as the waters cover the great and mighty deep (Isa. 11:9).

Chapter 19

Dancing in the Spirit as Victory

D avid danced with all his might before the Lord (2 Sam. 6:14). The Word is full of people dancing. Where dancing is mentioned in the Bible, it always signifies victory for the Lord's hosts. It was always done to glorify God. The Lord placed the spirit of power and love of the dance in the church. Wherever the Scripture speaks of dancing, it implies that people danced by inspiration and were moved by the Spirit, and the Lord was always pleased and smiled His approval. However, the Devil stole dancing away and made capital of it.

In these last days when God is pouring out His Spirit in great cloudbursts and tidal waves from the floodgates of heaven, and the great river of life is flooding our spirits and bodies, baptizing us with fire and resurrection life and divine energy, the Lord is doing *"his act*[s], *his strange act*[s]" (Isa. 28:21). There is dancing in the Spirit, speaking in other tongues, and many other operations and gifts. The Holy Spirit is confirming the last message of the coming King with great signs and wonders and miracles.

The Holy Spirit

If you read carefully what the Scriptures say about dancing, you will be surprised; you will see that singing, music, and dancing have a humble and holy place in the Lord's church:

> *Let them praise his name in the dance: let them sing praises unto him with the timbrel and harp.*
> (Ps. 149:3)

> *Praise him with the timbrel and dance: praise him with stringed instruments and organs.*
> (Ps. 150:4)

> *Then shall the virgin rejoice in the dance, both young men and old together.* (Jer. 31:13)

David Danced before the Lord

As I mentioned earlier, *"David danced before the LORD with all his might"* (2 Sam. 6:14). His wife Michal did not like it; she scolded him and made light of him. She said he was dancing before the maidens like a lewd fellow and made it seem as if he was base and low. But he answered, "I was not dancing before men, but before the Lord," showing that he had lost sight of the world and what they thought or said and was moved and controlled entirely by the Holy Spirit for the glory of God. All of the great company of people were blessed except Michal, and she was stricken with barrenness until the day of her death. (See 2 Samuel 6:12–23.) So you see, she sinned in making light of the power of God in the holy dance. Some do the same thing today, attributing it to the flesh or the Devil.

They always lose out, and many are in darkness until death.

Women Sang and Danced in Victory

Earlier in David's life, the news of his great victory—how he had killed the giant Goliath and destroyed the great army of the Philistines—spread quickly over the land. As the Israelite army was returning from the slaughter, the women came out of all the cities of Israel to meet King Saul. They were singing and dancing with great joy and instruments of music. Now, notice, in all their cities, the women went out in the streets and danced with their music. Men are not mentioned there, just maidens, and women danced unto the Lord in honor of God and the king, prompted by the Spirit of God to praise the Lord in the dance. It took courage to honor the king in this way, but the Lord smiled His approval by having it recorded by holy men of old and sent down to us in His precious Word. (See 1 Samuel 17:21–18:6.)

Moses' Sister Led Dancing

Another example of dancing in the Bible is when Miriam and the other Hebrew women danced after God saved the Israelites by parting the Red Sea and destroying the Egyptian armies.

And Miriam the prophetess, the sister of Aaron, took a timbrel in her hand; and all the women went out after her with timbrels and with dances. And Miriam answered them, Sing ye to the LORD, for he hath tri-umphed gloriously; the horse and his rider hath he thrown into the sea. (Exod. 15:20–21)

God has never done a greater miracle nor demonstrated His presence in so great a cloud of glory as at this time. While they were under the inspiration and light of His presence, their whole bodies and spirits going out in love, the whole multitude of women praised the Lord with dancing, shouting, and music. Miriam, the prophetess and leader, led them forth, and they sang a new song that had just been given by the Spirit and had never been sung before. Do you call that foolishness? No, they were praising the Lord in the dance and song as they were moving in and by the mighty power of God.

Moses also led the children of Israel in the same way, with music and dancing, singing this new song given by the Spirit for the occasion. (See Exodus 15:1–19.)

Dancing in the New Testament

In the New Testament, we find that joyful leaping sometimes accompanied healing. When the lame man was healed through the ministry of Peter and John, *"he leaping up stood, and walked, and entered with them into the temple, walking, and leaping, and praising God"* (Acts 3:8). In another instance, the apostle Paul said to a man who had been crippled since birth, *"Stand upright on thy feet"* (Acts 14:10). What was the result? *"He leaped and walked"* (v. 10).

We discover a reference to dancing in the Parable of the Prodigal Son. The elder son was in the field.

Dancing in the Spirit as Victory

When he came near the house, he heard music and dancing, and he asked, "What does all this mean?" They said, *"Thy brother is come; and thy father hath killed the fatted calf, because he hath received him safe and sound"* (Luke 15:27). "[The elder son] *was angry, and would not go in"* (v. 28), but the feast and rejoicing went on just the same. The Father said, *"It was meet that we should make merry, and be glad: for this thy brother was dead, and is alive again; and was lost, and is found"* (v. 32).

All will agree with me that this was an old-fashioned Holy Spirit revival. The lost son represents the sinner whom the Spirit has brought out of darkness into light; the saints are filled with the Spirit.

Dancing in the Spirit Today

So the Holy Spirit is falling on the saints of God today, and they are being used in the same way. Those who never danced one step are experts in the holy dance; those who do not know one note from another are expert musicians in playing many different instruments of music. Often, the sound of invisible instruments is heard from the platform; the sounds can be plainly heard all over the building. I say in the fear and presence of God: the singing and demonstration puts the fear of God on the people and causes a holy hush to come over them. The strange acts (Isa. 28:21) are occurring more and more. They show that they are something new and that Jesus is coming soon. The Lord is getting His bride ready to be translated and to dance and play at the great Marriage of the Lamb. This will soon take place, for the bride is making herself ready (Rev. 19:7).

The Holy Spirit

I was very slow to accept dancing in the Spirit, because I feared that it was of the flesh. However, I soon saw that it was the cloud of glory (see Exodus 16:10) over the people that brought forth the dancing and the playing of invisible instruments.

The sounds of sweet, heavenly music would often be heard in our meetings. Several times, I asked those in the congregation who heard this music coming from the platform (where they knew there were no instruments to be seen) to be honest and raise their hands. Many hands went up from saints and sinners. The stillness of death went over the people when they heard the sounds of music accompanied by the heavenly choir. Often, a message in tongues was given in one or more languages, along with the interpretation. As I saw the effect of the Holy Spirit on the people in convincing them that they were in the presence of God, I concluded that this was surely the Lord's strange work and His strange acts. (See Isaiah 28:21.)

I saw as many as nine of the most noted ministers dancing at one time on the platform. They danced singly, with their eyes closed. Often, some fell, slain by the mighty power of God. These things convinced me. I also saw men and women who have been crippled join in the dance with wonderful grace. One lady, who was on crutches for five years, got healed in her seat; afterward, she danced across the platform, singing heavenly music. I am reminded of the Scripture, "The virgins, the young men, and the old men all join in the dance together." (See Jeremiah 31:13.) Praise the Lord. *"Let us be glad and rejoice, and give honour to him: for the marriage of the Lamb is come, and his wife hath made herself ready"* (Rev. 19:7). The Lord is quickening our mortal bodies for the translation.

Chapter 20

Prepare for War

(Preached before World War I Began)

The following two quotations from Joel and Micah sound a little contradictory. I have heard people say so. But the statements refer to two different parties and times:

> *For, behold, in those days, and in that time, when I shall bring again the captivity of Judah and Jerusalem, I will also gather all nations, and will bring them down into the valley of Jehoshaphat....Proclaim ye this among the Gentiles; Prepare war, wake up the mighty men, let all the men of war draw near; let them come up: beat your plowshares into swords, and your pruninghooks into spears: let the weak say, I am strong.* (Joel 3:1–2, 9–10)

> *But in the last days it shall come to pass, that the mountain of the house of the LORD shall be established in the top of the mountains, and it shall be exalted above the hills; and people shall flow unto it. And many nations shall come, and say, Come, and let us go up to the mountain of the LORD, and to the house of*

the God of Jacob; and he will teach us of his ways, and we will walk in his paths: for the law shall go forth of Zion, and the word of the LORD from Jerusalem. And he shall judge among many people, and rebuke strong nations afar off; and they shall beat their swords into plowshares, and their spears into pruninghooks: nation shall not lift up a sword against nation, neither shall they learn war any more. But they shall sit every man under his vine and under his fig tree; and none shall make them afraid: for the mouth of the LORD of hosts hath spoken it.

(Mic. 4:1–4)

The first Scripture quotation under consideration, *"Beat your plowshares into swords, and your pruninghooks into spears"* (Joel 3:10), means "Get ready for battle," and it refers to this present time, a time of war. The second Scripture, *"Beat [your] swords into plowshares, and [your] spears into pruninghooks"* (Mic. 4:3), means "Get ready for a time of great farming."

The first one calls us to prepare for the greatest battle the world has ever heard of; the other refers to the time when war will be no more.

"Prepare for war; wake up the mighty men of war; let the nations gather together for battle" (see Joel 3:2, 9) refers to this time of the end that we are now living in, when the time of the Gentiles (Rom. 11:25) has been completed or is coming to a close.

A Mighty Man of War

You see the awful slaughter, massacre, and deadly hatred that is causing the nations to kill and destroy each other. God has risen up like a *"mighty...man of war"*

(Isa. 42:13). He will roar and shout out from Jerusalem (Joel 3:16) until all nations are gathered in deadly combat, until the blood flows like a river.

In the text in Joel, the call is primarily to the Holy Land, where the great Battle of God Almighty will be fought. This is the Battle of the great Day of God, when the angel is standing in the sun calling all the fowls of the air to come to the supper of the great God, to eat the flesh of all the mighty men, the great men of the world, and the rich men. They are invited to eat and drink the blood and get fat on the flesh, on the carcasses of kings and princes of the world, who will soon fall in the *"notable day of the Lord"* (Acts 2:20). (See Revelation 19:17–18.)

The Lord will awaken and shout out as a *"man of war"* (Isa. 42:13). He will *"roar out of Zion, and utter his voice from Jerusalem; and the heavens and the earth shall shake"* (Joel 3:16) when the nations are gathering for this great Battle with the Lamb and His army from heaven.

The apostle John wrote,

And I saw heaven opened, and behold a white horse; and he that sat upon him....His eyes were as a flame of fire, and on his head were many crowns....And he was clothed with a vesture dipped in blood....And the armies which were in heaven followed him upon white horses, clothed in fine linen, white and clean.
(Rev. 19:11–14)

Oh, praise the Lord! Let me give you the background of this verse. The saints have been translated to heaven. The Marriage of the Lamb and His bride has taken place, with shouting and hallelujahs that have shaken all heaven and earth. The great Marriage Supper, with all its grandeur and glory and greatness, is over. The saints have been with the Lord, executing judgments on the earth during the awful Tribulation.

Now the cup of wickedness is full. The God of heaven has been defied long enough. He has stood up in His wrath. All nations of the earth are gathering to the *"valley of Jehoshaphat"* (Joel 3:2). The Antichrist has gathered his army and is about to destroy God's children. The *"KING OF KINGS AND LORD OF LORDS"* (Rev. 19:16), with all His armies of heaven, comes riding in triumph, down through the skies. Enoch saw the Lord coming with *"ten thousands of his saints"* (Jude 14). All the armies will gather together against Jerusalem to fight, but then the Lord will come from heaven and fight this great Battle. The saints do not have to fight: the Lord Himself does the fighting.

Millennial Kingdom

Following this, the millennial kingdom will be set up, and Satan will be chained during the thousand years. During this time, the curse and its effects, including all weeds, thistles, and anything that would produce disease and the like, will have been taken away. *"They shall not hurt nor destroy in all my holy mountain"* (Isa. 11:9). The time is coming when they will cease to make war, and the Devil will be taken out of the hearts of the people.

Today, people are just like wild beasts that are thirsting for each other's blood. They are burying the living and the dead together. Pestilence also has already begun its deadly havoc.

Have you ever heard of a great war breaking out so quickly, the way it has in Europe? For years past, the most talented men have been inventing weapons in order to see who could make the most deadly ones.

God has been holding back the tidal waves and other destructive forces. His angel has shouted, "Wait until the servants of God are sealed with the seal of God." (See Revelation 7:3.)

The chapters in the book of Joel have been divided poorly. The first verses of the third chapter are a continuation of the last verses of the second chapter and should not be separated from them.

"And it shall come to pass in the last days, saith God, I will pour out of my Spirit" (Acts 2:17, quoting Joel 2:28). God will baptize with the Holy Spirit and disseminate the power of the holy people.

God says, "I will rise up in My wrath in that Day." (See Joel 2:1–11.) When the judgments of God are in the earth, some will repent. (See verse 32.) *"In the last days, saith God, I will pour out of my Spirit."* God says to wake up the heathen (Joel 3:9, 12).

God is sealing His saints, but that sealing time is pretty nearly over. That fact that the saints speak in *"new tongues"* (Mark 16:17) is a sign that the Lord is coming.

The power of the holy people will be disseminated. These are they who are clay in the Potter's hands. They are just clay, having no control over themselves at all. God Almighty speaks through them: *"With stammering lips and another tongue will* [I] *speak to this people....Yet they* [will] *not hear"* (Isa. 28:11–12).

Proclaim and tell it to the people. *"Blow ye the trumpet in Zion, and sound an alarm in my holy mountain"* (Joel 2:1). What is the danger? The Day of the Lord is coming; it is near at hand.

God's people are blowing the trumpet. They are sounding the alarm in Zion. What is the signal of danger? The great Day of the Lord is near.

It is time for the saints to get this knowledge, if they do not already know it. How can we give the signal if we do not know? How can we warn the people of danger?

If they escape when the sword is coming, good. But warn them anyhow. If we do not warn them, their blood will be on our hands. Wake up the heathen. Call up your mighty men. Call the soldiers into line. Get them ready. Get the weapons of war ready for the world's great conflict. There never has been anything like it, nor will there ever be again.

The nations are continually building new warships and manufacturing so many deadly weapons. Each nation is trying to build the largest ships and invent the most deadly weapons. Yet they are still crying, "Peace, peace." Right in the midst of this false peace and security, death and war and destruction have come like a whirlwind.

Men will be hunting around in the farmyards, old barns, stables, sheds, and everywhere for old plowshares and pruning hooks—for everything that they can beat into swords and spears to kill their neighbors with. Your neighbor will be hunting around for a piece of old steel to kill his neighbor with.

The time is coming in this glorious America when parties and factions will rise up—labor against capital, and other parties and factions. At that time, no one will be able to buy or sell unless they have the mark of the beast (Rev. 13:16–17). It will mean death, but to have the mark of the beast will mean the *"second death"* (Rev. 2:11).

There will be no safety or hiding place for him who goes out or in: *"As if a man did flee from a lion, and a bear met him; or went into the house, and leaned his hand on the wall, and a serpent bit him"* (Amos 5:19).

It is implied that the land will be infested with poisonous serpents, reptiles, and insects and that they will be turned loose among the people, with their deadly power to bite, sting, and destroy. So if a person runs away from the sword and pestilence and tries to hide in the house, he will rest his hand on the wall and be bitten by a deadly serpent. There will be no safety for him who goes in or out.

There will be awful, deadly hatred among the people, and they will be banded together hand in hand. They will make weapons of steel with which to kill and destroy one another. It is time to wake up from the sleep of death and call on God to give you life.

According to the Word of God and the signs of the times, we are now living in the commencement of these awful times, when many who read these lines will see a great deal more than I have written. You and your children will go down in death or go through this dreadful time of trouble, such as never has been or ever will be again.

Many of the best Bible students say that the eleventh chapter of Daniel refers to the Sultan, or ruling powers of Turkey. *"And he shall plant the tabernacles of his palace between the seas in the glorious holy mountain; yet he shall come to his end, and none shall help him"* (Dan.

11:45). They think that the book of Obadiah also refers to him.

The passage in Daniel does not refer to the Antichrist, for he will not be revealed or take his power until after the Hinderer is taken away (see 2 Thessalonians 2:7)—until Christ takes out a people for His name from among the Gentiles, until He comes and takes His bride.

He will come to his end in the *"time of the end"* (Dan. 11:40). At that time, Michael, the great prince, will stand up for God's people, and all whose names are written in the Book of Life will be delivered. (See Daniel 12:1.) The wise, who will know these things, will *"shine as the brightness of the firmament"* (12:3).

It is reported that the Turks are building a large palace, or building; they are keeping it quiet and will not tell anyone what it is for. *"He shall plant the tabernacles of his palace between the seas in the glorious holy mountain; yet he shall come to his end, and none shall help him"* (Dan. 11:45). But he will not stay there very long; little by little, he will go down until he is entirely destroyed.

The Holy Land was to be trodden down by the Gentiles until the *"time of the end"* (8:17). Then, and at that time, Christ will come. The Jews will flock to Jerusalem and again possess the Holy Land.

Most of those who will go through the Tribulation will have had enough, and they will be ready to listen to the voice of the *"false prophet"* (Rev. 16:13).

If the angels are loosed (see Revelation 19:14–15), it will not be long before we take our flight. When these things begin to come fast, we will soon be taken out of the world. The worst trouble will come after the saints are taken out. The Antichrist will deny the blessed Christ and cause people to take his mark or be put to death. Those who do not go with Christ will have to go through this or go down in it.

Jesus will come to take a people out for His name, for His bride. He will come and take her away to the heavens. The great Marriage Supper will take place, after which the saints will be sitting with Christ on His throne and helping to execute judgment during this awful Tribulation.

Look at the terrible death and carnage and destruction you will experience if you do not go up with the bridal company. Those who go up when Christ comes are the Lamb's wife. Then He will return to build up the *"waste places of Jerusalem"* (Isa. 52:9). The soil will all be fertile then, and the people will not need to do much work. During the Millennium, it will be like a holy camp meeting all the time.

The first time Jesus returns, no one will see Him but the bride. The world hates her and cares nothing for her, and Jesus is going to take her away. Christ will come as quickly as the lightning flashes from the east to the west. (See Matthew 24:27.) Just that quickly, He will snatch His bridal company away, while the world sleeps in a drunken stupor.

But the next time He comes, all will know it. Every knee will bow and every tongue will confess that Jesus Christ is Lord (Phil. 2:10–11). Every eye will see Him (Rev. 1:7), and every slanderous tongue will have to confess before the world that the saints were God's chosen vessels. (See Revelation 3:9.)

This honor belongs to the saints. The world will have to confess that we were right and they were wrong.

The Holy Spirit

God is very proud of His bride. Children of God now deny themselves many of the things of the world. Yet we are heirs of the kingdom, even though many of us are poor in this world and are experiencing hard times. There is going to be a change in this old world. God is calling you to see this. Don't go a step further. Don't step over the mangled body of Christ any more, or it may be the last time.

As I said, the first time Christ returns, the bride will be caught away; the second time, the saints will come riding on white horses. (See Revelation 19:14.) Jesus will stand on Mount Olivet, and those who pierced Him will see Him (Rev. 1:7). You now know, down in your hearts, that Jesus is the Christ, that every believer present in this meeting is in earnest, that we hear something more than natural men hear. The wisdom we receive comes from God, who gives liberally. This has been my prayer more than anything else: "Give me wisdom." Why, even a blind man can see by looking at the signs of the times. Daniel said that the wise will know when the Lord comes.

You may say, "I don't believe." You just don't want to believe, and that Day will overtake you as a thief in the night. None of the wicked will understand the signs of Jesus' coming. You who are children of the light will know, and that Day will not overtake you unexpectedly. (See 1 Thessalonians 5:4–5.) God gave Daniel a picture of those who belong to the lost world, none of whom will know when He comes.

Who are the wise? Those who know the time of the Lord's coming. *"They that turn many to righteousness* [will shine] *as the stars"* (Dan. 12:3). But *"they that be wise shall shine as the brightness of the firmament"* (v. 3). They who are wise will know.

Prepare for War

This is a wonderful message. Now you can have your choice. The greatest vengeance and pent-up wrath of God will be poured out on those who take the mark of the Antichrist. If we trust in God, we can have faith so that none of these things will hurt us.

Look up, dear children of the living God. Look up; our redemption is near (Luke 21:28), even at the door (Matt. 24:33). Oh, God, help us to awaken the sleeping virgins (see Matthew 25:5) and tell them to flee to Christ, to get the baptism of the Holy Spirit, to get sealed with the *"Spirit of promise"* (Eph. 1:13), to get ready to take the flight in the air.

Oh, accept the invitation to the Marriage Supper of the Lamb. He will come like a flash of lightning from the east. We will go in a moment. We will arise to meet Him in the sky.

Don't be looking to the grave. Look up. *"Behold, He cometh"* (Rev. 1:7). *"Glory to God in the highest"* (Luke 2:14). Come, O Redeemer; come quickly.

Chapter 21

Fear God, and Give Him Glory

And I saw another angel fly in the midst of heaven,
having the everlasting gospel to preach unto them
that dwell on the earth, and to every nation,
and kindred, and tongue, and people, saying with a
loud voice, Fear God, and give glory to him;
for the hour of his judgment is come: and worship
him that made heaven, and earth, and the sea,
and the fountains of waters.
—Revelation 14:6–7

O ur text describes certain things John saw in his Revelation. He was carried away in a trance, and he was not hypnotized, either. He saw an angel. He did not simply think so, but he saw it, flying *"in the midst of heaven, having the everlasting gospel to preach"* and saying, *"Fear God, and give glory to him."*

The image of an angel flying through the earth, preaching the everlasting Gospel, applies to us today in a wonderful way. We are living in the last days, right at the end of this glorious dispensation. God is calling out a people from among men, preparing the bride whom Jesus is coming to receive as His own. God is calling His servants for the ministry of the Gospel of His kingdom. They go over the land with swiftness. They are called eagles. The eagle has great power, and it soars over every difficulty. It is so with God's children in these days. God gives us strength and courage that has never existed before.

We are sent as angels to sound the trumpet. When God calls, we have to go, skipping across the ocean, running, flying, soaring over the world. Nothing can pull us down. God is calling us to give this old world the last call. He is taking men and women whom He can trust with His power to show forth His goods to the world. A traveling salesman shows his goods and secures orders. If he did not show his goods, he would not get the orders. People want to see the goods before they purchase them.

So God calls us to show the samples. We are not only to tell what God can do, but to put Him to the test and show what He can do. We must be clothed with the power of the King, showing such signs and wonders as the world has never seen. That will put the fear of the Lord on all those who see and hear.

Never before have we had a greater responsibility. The message is, *"Fear God, and give glory to him; for the hour of his judgment is come.'* Worship God, *'which made heaven, and earth, the sea, and all that therein is'* (Ps 146:6). Worship Him as never before."

There are as many gods being worshipped in America today as there are among the heathen. The God of heaven is left in the shade, and the Lord Jesus

Fear God, and Give Him Glory

Christ is thrown down by many professing Christians. Give glory to Him, Him, Him, the God of heaven. Worship Him, *"and give glory to him; for the hour of his judgment is come."* That time is here. *"Fear God, and give glory to him."*

What is the message we are to give? Jesus is coming soon. God has given out the invitation to the Marriage Supper of His Son. We are invited to the Feast, and we are having our wedding garments made. There is everything to coax the bride away from her father's house, from everything that binds her, and to draw her to the Bridegroom.

"Gather yourselves together" (Zeph. 2:1). Those of you who follow Him, gather yourselves together—you who are despised and rejected. (See verse 1.) All men speak evil of this "sect." (See Acts 28:22.) Seek righteousness, meekness, and power from God. Hide away.

Watchman, what do you see of the morning? Glory to God! The sun is rising in the East. He is coming! What about the night? The night is coming soon. Death and destruction are coming; the judgments of God are coming. *"Blow ye the trumpet in Zion"* (Joel 2:1) and sound the alarm in the Holy Mountain (v. 1). Let all the people tremble.

Why are the people going to get alarmed and tremble? What is the danger? The armies of the Devil are gathering. Hide, hide away in the rock from the wrath of God that is coming upon the earth. My God, warn the people! Let them tremble on account of their sins. We have to blow the trumpet, the signal of danger. We have to give the warning and let the people know. The angelic choir is getting ready. His people are being trained down here to sing the song of the redeemed.

The Holy Spirit

(See Revelation 14:3.) May the people tremble; may the fear of God come upon them. There is a great Day coming, a Day of black darkness, black as midnight. God's judgment is going to burst upon this earth. Give the signal of danger. The great Day of the Lord is coming; it is near at hand. He is at the door. (See Matthew 24:33.) If we know it, help us to tell it!

The ancient cities had great walls around them, and watchmen were placed day and night upon the walls. If they saw an army approaching, an enemy coming, or any danger threatening, they blew the trumpet, giving the warning to the men of war in the city who understood the signal, so that the people could escape. If the watchmen did not give the signal, the blood of the people was on their heads.

Watchmen, if you do not warn the people and the Enemy comes in and takes them, their blood will be upon your heads. God puts us upon the walls of Zion. Jesus is coming in this generation. The young people will not be old when He comes. According to His Word, the time is near. We are all either for Him or against Him. How can you give the signal of danger if you do not know it? Worship God, and give glory to Him, the God of heaven. If you blow the trumpet right, it will arouse the people. Then if they continue sleeping, your hands will be free from blood.

There never was such a responsibility on the people of God as there is today. There never was such a time for Jesus Christ to be lifted up as He is today. Gods of science and nature and other gods are on the earth today. At a gathering of twenty-three ministers in Boston, only three accepted the divinity of Christ. We have to drop all side issues and hobbies, everything else but Jesus; we must lift up Jesus.

Fear God, and Give Him Glory

In these days, our Lord is being crucified a thousand times worse than on the cross. In these days, His honor and His glory are at stake. Stand by Him, and defend His holy name. Hold up the fountain of Calvary that is opened wide; it cleanses from the effects of sin. It has power today, flowing from the wounded side of Jesus. Let us stand by Him in the battle against the world, the flesh, and the Devil. Men may call us every name that can be invented—hypnotists, fanatics, and crackpots—trying to strike those who are stepping out on God's promises. How the heart of Jesus must bleed! If we stand firm with Him, He will let the people know the work is of God. Stand firm; set your face like flint (Isa. 50:7). Prove the Word; He says He will stand by us to deliver us in the hour of temptation and in the hour of tribulation that is coming on the earth. Be true to Him; hold up the Atonement and the power of the blood. He will save us from the black darkness that is settling over the world.

We have to stand by Him and lift up Jesus, though men and devils howl and speak against Him and the wonderful works of the blessed Holy Spirit. Can He find messengers, men and women, who will interpret the Word correctly and show what the mighty power of God is? He says that if we will stand by Him now and blow the trumpet, the Word of God will encircle the earth. God will be here to judge His people, and the glory of heaven will be brought down to fight our battles. Let us lift up Jesus.

Don't talk about side issues; don't get a bone of contention and talk about it. When people know Him, they will know what to do, what to wear, how to get married, and how to live when they are married. Preach Jesus. Glory to God! People will not change their ideas to please you. God Almighty has to show them. These things break up meetings, and the people lose their power. Lift up Jesus. It is not by might or by power; it is Almighty God doing the work (Zech. 4:6). We must show forth what He is doing. Let us stand by Him during this short time when the command goes forth to blow the trumpet.

The great Day of the Lord is near at hand; it is at the door (Matt. 24:33). Give the signal of danger, and He will back it up by signs and wonders. If we are preaching the Word, we must have the signs and wonders to get people to believe in Him.

People are worshipping a mystical god; they are following *"doctrines of devils"* (1 Tim. 4:1). The wrath of God must come upon those who follow these things, and the blood will come up to the horses' bridles (Rev. 14:20). God is holding back the four winds (Rev. 7:1) to give us a chance to blow this trumpet, and He will back it up with power. The time is near at hand. There are temples of idols set up in this land, and a man sets himself up as if he is God. (See 2 Thessalonians 2:3–4.) They are getting ready; everywhere, federations are forming.

Don't go into these federations; keep out of them. Don't be afraid of their threats. Fear God, for the hour of His judgment is at hand. Can you not see these things? People are preaching the fatherhood of God and the brotherhood of man, but they are leaving out the blood of Christ entirely. Don't be afraid of their threats. Fear God; He will deliver. We see these things; we see them everywhere. Christ is at hand. Worship the God of heaven.

Who will stand for Jesus, the lowly Nazarene? Who will stand for Him when everyone is pointing the finger of derision? There are millions of professing Christians today who are denying the Lord who bought them. They deny the divinity of Christ, and they deny the power of the Holy Spirit. You can have the knowledge of these things if the blood of Jesus cleanses you. You may feed the poor and all that, but if you do not have the Spirit of God, all that you do outside of Jesus Christ will never build a ladder to take you to heaven. You cannot go there except through Christ. If you are in the flesh, and the Spirit of God does not dwell in you (compare Romans 8:9), then you are a reprobate. Yet, little children, you do know God (1 John 2:13). Praise His name. Give God the glory.

God has revealed by the Spirit that the Laodicean church will be spewed out (Rev. 3:14–16). The Sardian church has a reputation for being alive, but they are spiritually dead (v. 1). They have a beautiful outside form, but they deny the power of the Holy Spirit; *"from such turn away"* (2 Tim 3:5). They do not know the Holy Spirit or the blood that bought them. They stand off to one side and say that rather than being under the power of the Spirit, people are hypnotized, mesmerized, or drunk—as some said about the disciples on the Day of Pentecost. They do not want to investigate; they are afraid of being called fools by the world. I would rather be a fool in God's hands than a fool in front of the Devil. Wouldn't you?

David danced before the ark of the Lord with all his might (2 Sam. 6:14), yet they call us fanatics because we dance. May God give us more fanatics. Don't you see the darkness in the land? None of these people, judging by their actions, know anything about the Holy Spirit. When they come near us, there is a fear on them; they don't want to believe it. May God help us to know

The Holy Spirit

the difference between being mesmerized and being under the power of God. It is the power of God, yet they call it hypnotism when they see people laid out under His mighty power.

Don't you see how little they know of Jesus? He set us the example. He cast out demons and healed the sick. He sent the Holy Spirit down upon His disciples, and they staggered like drunken men and spoke in tongues (Acts 2:1–4). They were *"drunken, but not with wine; they stagger, but not with strong drink"* (Isa. 29:9). This is the way today. John the Baptist prophesied that Jesus would baptize with the Holy Spirit and fire (Matt. 3:11). What do you know about that? When people see the Holy Spirit working, they say we are crazy.

God's people are alive. Give glory to God, and worship Him, for the hour of the Judgment is at hand. You see some people worshipping a dead Christ, giving heed to *"doctrines of men"* (Col. 2:22) and *"doctrines of devils"* (1 Tim. 4:1). There is a power in education, wealth, and fine sermons. Yet may God help us to preach in the power of the Holy Spirit. They set Christ aside. If they had the blood of Christ applied to their hearts, how they would love God! Then they would know the power of the blood and the power of the Holy Spirit.

Christ said: *"'I* [will] *send the promise of my Father'* (Luke 24:49) and *'ye shall receive power, after that the Holy Ghost is come upon you'* (Acts 1:8). Then you will work miracles. Preach My Word, and I will be with you." (See Matthew 28:20.) He is with us. If you will believe correctly, you will cast out demons—legions are all around us. You will *"lay hands on the sick, and they shall recover"* (Mark 16:18). They will not be mesmerized, as some claim. Praise God!

Fear God, and Give Him Glory

Quit your grumbling, and get the experience of the baptism in the Holy Spirit so that you can praise God. Many make fun of the work of the Holy Spirit. You can see it in the city papers. God's work isn't being presented in its true light; it is being presented in a foolish, sensational way, to make people think it is of the Devil.

"When the Son of man cometh, shall he find faith on the earth?" (Luke 18:8). He will find only a little flock watching for Him. On the Day of Pentecost, Peter did not say, "There is no power here." He said it was the Holy Spirit, spoken of by the prophet Joel. (See Acts 2:14–18.) The people there saw the tongues of fire; they heard the sound as of a *"rushing mighty wind"* (vv. 2–3). It was the Holy Spirit, and He is here tonight. Be careful how you speak against Him. He is in these acts of healing and in the tongues. There is great power among the people who are giving the last warning before Jesus comes.

May God help us as never before to see Jesus in the power of His blood. Let us give Jesus the preeminence. Let us preach Jesus and the Resurrection. Show He is coming by the signs, by the power to deliver the people. You know He is coming. Show the signs, and you won't have to do much preaching. The people will see the miracles, and many will be saved. Let us lift up Jesus as never before. Let the people see nothing but Jesus; they will soon drop everything that is unclean and go higher and higher and deeper still.

May God put His seal upon these truths in our hearts. The crisis is nearer than anyone thinks. Lift up Jesus, and God will show people the truth. God must show them by working through you. Glory to His name!

Chapter 22

Set Your House in Order

Thus saith the LORD, Set thine house in order:
for thou shalt die, and not live.
—Isaiah 38:1

My prayer is that the Lord will stop every sinner in his tracks who reads these words. I pray that you will understand the warning in the text to mean you, that you will take the nearest way to the Cross and throw yourself at the bleeding feet of the dying Lamb of God, and that you will let Him cleanse and wash out all the sin and filth from your heart and mind. I pray that you will let the Lord Jesus come in and take possession of your house, your self— that He will fill you with His love and presence, be the keeper of the house, and speak to You, so that you may obey like a dear child. His sheep hear His voice. When He leads, they follow (John 10:27).

Jesus has spoken to you many times by His Spirit and told you that this world is not your home and that it is not all of life to live or all of death to die, but that after death comes the Judgment. He has shown you that you are a sinner, lost and undone, that the wrath of God hangs over you. If you die in your sins, it will be an awful thing to *"fall into the hands of the living God"* (Heb. 10:31). If you go on in your sins, you will be arrested by the Sheriff of Heaven and be bound hand and foot; you will be cast into *"outer darkness,"* where the inhabitants weep and wail and gnash their teeth (Matt. 8:12). The Lord has told you that the time will come when you will cry for mercy. Yet the mercy door will be closed, and God will not hear you. He will laugh and mock at your fears and calamity. He will say, *"Depart from me, ye cursed, into everlasting fire,"* a place *"prepared for the devil and his angels"* (Matt. 25:41).

Heaven was prepared for you, but if you are not pure in heart, the pearly gates will be closed against you. This world will be wrapped in flames; it will burn as pitch and tar, and the wicked will be swept off into destruction.

In view of the terrible doom the text implies, make the preparation at once. You will have to die someday, and there is no repentance in the grave. As you go down in death, you will rise in the Judgment. Death is coming; that terrible eternity is before you! Before the sun rises or sets again, you may be cold in death, and your soul may be lost.

The Pale Horse

You will soon hear the clatter of the feet of the pale horse and his rider, the monster Death (Rev. 6:8), bearing down upon you. You will have a race with the pale horse, and he will run you down into the cold, icy river of death. You will die soon and meet your God, whether you are ready or not. The Lord says, "Prepare for death, *'for thou shalt die.'"*

"As I live, saith the Lord GOD, I have no pleasure in the death of the wicked; but that the wicked turn from his way and live" (Ezek. 33:11).

Hear Him call. Seek the Lord while He may be found. Call upon Him while He is near (Isa. 55:6). *"He will not always chide: neither will he keep his anger forever"* (Ps. 103:9). God has warned you through the rolling thunder, the flashing lightning, and the cyclone. The voice of God has spoken to you, saying, "Take warning; fly to Christ, and seek shelter from the storms of the great Judgment Day."

The Day of His wrath is coming, and who will be able to stand (Mal. 3:2)? Every funeral procession you see tells you that you, too, must soon die. Are you ready? When you stood by the bedside of one struggling in death or looked on the face in the coffin, the Lord said to you, "Prepare for death, and follow Me."

Every autumn you look upon the withered flowers and falling leaves. They tell you of death. Death is written on the breezes. Everything points to death and shows you that you will soon be laid away in the silent city of the dead and will soon be forgotten by the living.

Withering Leaves, Fading Flowers

You hear the solemn moaning of the winds through the leafy trees. They say to you, "This world is not your home; you did not come here to stay forever." Seek a home in heaven—a house not built with hands

The Holy Spirit

(2 Cor. 5:1), *"whose builder and maker is God"* (Heb. 11:10)—where you will soon meet all your loved ones, to be forever with the Lord.

When you walk over the withered flowers and faded leaves, and as they rustle beneath your feet, the voice of God speaks to you, saying, "You are passing away. You will soon be lying underneath the ground, and you will soon be forgotten." The thoughtless throng will walk over your moldering form and think no more of you than you do of the dead leaves you are crushing beneath your feet.

Dear reader, if you have not given your heart to Jesus, drop to your knees, confess your sins to Him, and accept Him as your personal Savior. Do not rise until the light of heaven shines down in your soul and you know you are saved. If you do not, you will soon find yourself swept out on the shores of eternity, lost, lost forever!

The Great Judgment Morning

I dreamed that the Great Judgment morning
    Had dawned, and the trumpet had blown;
I dreamed that the nations had gathered
    To Judgment before the White Throne.
From the throne came a bright-shining angel
    And stood on the land and the sea,
And swore with his hand raised to heaven,
    That time was no longer to be.

And, oh, what a weeping and wailing
    When the lost ones were told of their fate;
They cried for the rocks and the mountains,
    They prayed but their prayers were too late.

Set Your House in Order

The rich man was there, but his money
  Had melted and vanished away;
A pauper he stood in the Judgment,
  His debts were too heavy to pay.
The great man was there, but his greatness
  When death came was left far behind,
The angel that opened the records
  Not a trace of his greatness could find.

The widow was there and the orphans,
  God heard and remembered their cries;
No sorrow in heaven forever,
  God wiped all the tears from their eyes.
The gambler was there and the drunkard,
  And the man who had sold them the drink,
With the people who gave him the license—
  Together in hell they did sink.

The moral man came to the Judgment,
  But his self-righteous rags would not do;
The men who had crucified Jesus
  Had passed off as moral men, too.
The soul that had put off salvation—
  "Not tonight; I'll get saved by and by;
No time now to think of religion!"
  At last they had found time to die.

Epilogue

Since my last book, *Signs and Wonders,* * was written, I have held meetings in a number of places, including some of the largest cities out West. In regard to our meeting in Sidney, Iowa, one of the local papers had this to report about the work:

> The crowd of spectators Sunday night was said to have been the largest ever seen at the city park on any occasion. They come back here sick and maimed, on crutches and in wheelchairs, and go away apparently sound and well and shouting hosannas to the Most High. Call it hypnotism or what you will, there is no dodging the fact that Mrs. Etter is exerting a power over these people that passeth common understanding. We give it up; we have no solution.

In addition, here are a few words taken from the *Fremont* (County) *Herald:*

> The big camp meeting is still in progress at the park and is more than ever the main topic of

[8] See Maria Woodworth-Etter, *Signs and Wonders* (New Kensington, PA: Whitaker House, 1997).

conversation on the streets and in the majority of the homes in Sidney. Each day brings a number of people from a distance, on the train and in autos. The local reporter asked for the names of some of the people who were registered from a distance, but the joke was on her, for there were so many that the paper couldn't print them all. For the first time we can remember, a religious gathering has driven out a good show, and before they went, the members of the company, which was booked for the whole week before last at the opera house, went over to the camp meeting to see what had taken their crowds.

These meetings stirred this little town and its surrounding territory as nothing had ever done before. I remember that, on a Sunday, just as we had dismissed the meeting, the power of God fell on a little boy with a speech impediment. He was about twelve years old. He got up and walked back and forth on the platform, giving messages in tongues and exhorting the people to get down and pray, pray, pray! He would take his handkerchief and wipe off the perspiration and tears from his face, stamp his little feet, and plead with the people to get down and pray, hide away in God, and get ready for His coming. In a very short time, he had every saint and nearly all the sinners down on their knees, weeping and calling upon God.

From this little place, we headed for San Francisco, California. The saints in Salt Lake City, Utah, just a few in number, begged us to stop off at their city and hold a meeting. We did so, and we held a three-week campaign. God broke through the Mormon ranks. People got saved, healed, and baptized. I believe that if I could have stayed longer, the whole city would have been shaken. We held the meetings in the building in which prizefights were held. On the same blood-stained mat where the prizefights were being staged, sinners were weeping their way through to God, staining it with their tears. Surely this piece of canvas will be a witness for and against some people in the Day of Judgment. At this place, the glory of God was seen with the natural eye by about a dozen of the saints. The pastor, an evangelist, myself, and other Christian workers were among those who saw the wonderful sight—the glory of God like a cloud resting over the meeting.

New Tabernacle Built

I am very eager for the saints and the dear people everywhere to know why we have built the tabernacle in Indianapolis, Indiana. The Lord appeared before me in the night and brought the building before me. He told me to arise and build a house for the Lord. The message and plan came so forcibly before me that I knew it was the voice of God. I rose the next morning, laid the message and plan before my secretary, and told him that we must proceed at once to make arrangements for the building.

In about two months' time, the building was finished. We have a large, neat, comfortable tabernacle. Indianapolis is a large, beautiful, centralized city, a city that is easily accessible to the saints in the North, South, East, and West. All those traveling across the continent can conveniently stop off here. The Lord has made it plain that this place is prepared to call the saints together from all parts of the world and to get a special enduement with power from on high. It is qualified to do the last work and to get the last call, to gather in the hungry souls, to get them sealed with the seal of the living God and ready for the Rapture.

A brother in Canada wrote me that God showed him this is to be a lighthouse, that He is going to send the light out all over the world from this place.

God has put His seal on the building and the work in many ways. He has revealed to the saints in different places about establishing a work here. Some have had visions of the building before it was built.

The power and presence of the Lord have been present in a marvelous way from the first meeting, confirming the work with signs and miracles, and in a special manner displaying the supernatural. The heavenly choir has come forth many times accompanied by heavenly instruments. Angels have been seen and heard singing by many saints. The glory of God and Jesus has been seen over the pulpit and all over the tabernacle at times. Last Sunday, a brother saw Jesus appear on a throne over the platform. Streams of light and glory were going out from Him all over the building. This brother's face fairly shone as he testified to it. The next night, two sisters saw Him at about the same time. One was newly baptized. She saw Him close to her; the other one saw Him as He walked across the platform.

The saints are convinced that this is the time for God to do a mighty work. He wants to raise up workers who will go out under the anointing and in the unity of the Spirit to carry the work everywhere. We feel and know that this is the last call. What we do, we must do quickly.

Epilogue

Many People Healed, Saved, and Baptized

A Mrs. E. A. Moore was instantly healed of a stroke of paralysis that she had suffered. Her right side and bowels were paralyzed. For some days after the stroke, she was speechless, too. They brought her to the meeting and had to assist her onto the platform. When the prayer of faith was offered for her, she got up, walked, and gave praises to God. She demonstrated publicly that she had the use of the right side of her body again. Her neighbors consider it a great miracle. This sister has been well ever since. At another time, a black sister was brought in much the same condition. She was prayed for, and she came in about two weeks later without a sign of lameness.

Saints have come in from all the surrounding states, received what they came for, and gone back rejoicing. Some of them have come back the second time, bringing others with them.

A brother from Marcellus, Michigan, came down and got spiritually revived. He went back home and brought his mother, wife, two children, and some friends to the meeting. They all received the baptism of the Holy Spirit.

A number of hungry souls came in from Louisville, Kentucky. They also received the baptism.

One man came in from Virginia to get healed of tuberculosis. He got healed and baptized. When he got back home, he sent his wife here to be prayed for. She got healed and also received the baptism.

One brother came in from Oklahoma; he had been seeking the baptism of the Holy Spirit for a year. After he was here only a few days, he received a marvelous baptism. When he got back home, he sent his son, daughter, and a friend to Indianapolis. They also received the baptism; only the daughter was a little doubtful about whether she had received the baptism in its fullness.

As nearly as I can tell, about fifty have already followed Jesus in the ordinance of water baptism at this writing. When the first candidates were baptized in water in the baptistry, God put His seal on the ceremony in a wonderful way. Messages in tongues with interpretations came forth, and a number of the saints standing close by were slain in the Spirit and lay as though they were dead, under the mighty power of God. A group of angels was seen over the baptistry and was heard singing while the ceremony went on.

So many people are sending in handkerchiefs to have us pray over and anoint them that I believe I will say a few words about this part of my ministry. As in the days of Paul (see Acts 19:11–12), God is healing people through pieces of cloth. We have prayed for thousands of these cloths and handkerchiefs and have sent them out in the name of Jesus. The reports come in daily, and it is wonderful how God heals people through them. Others get saved and baptized in the Spirit.

I was just given a testimony from a man from Missouri. In this testimony, a man who had had tuberculosis for fifteen years, and whose relatives had all died from it, was instantly healed when an anointed handkerchief was placed on his body. He has had no more hemorrhages or coughing, and damp atmospheres have no effect whatsoever upon him anymore. He had been told by the doctors that he would not live three months if he stopped taking his medicine. This is only one out of the many such testimonies that we receive.

Epilogue

Now my prayer is that God will greatly bless this book. It will be prayed over as it goes out in the vineyard. What we do for Jesus and His cause must be done very quickly, because the coming of Jesus is right upon us. *"The Spirit and the bride say, Come....And let him that is athirst come. And whosoever will, let him take the water of life freely* (Rev. 22:17). Yes, *"come, Lord Jesus"* (v. 20). Amen.

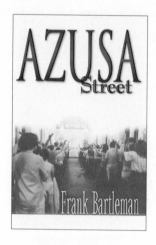

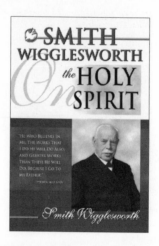

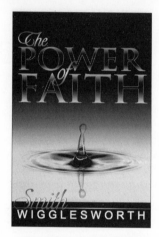

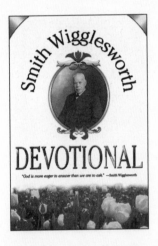

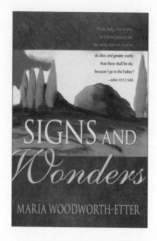